THIS BOOK BELONGS TO

Verily I say unto you, all those who receive my
gospel are sons and daughters in my kingdom.
Doctrine and Covenants 25:1

DAUGHTERS
in My Kingdom

THE HISTORY AND WORK
OF RELIEF SOCIETY

Published by
The Church of Jesus Christ of Latter-day Saints
Salt Lake City, Utah

RELIEF SOCIETY

PURPOSES

*Increase faith and
personal righteousness*

*Strengthen families
and homes*

*Seek out and help
those in need*

Contents

A Message from the
First Presidency

Dear Sisters:

In grateful recognition of the blessing of Relief Society in the lives of Church members, we have directed the preparation of *Daughters in My Kingdom: The History and Work of Relief Society.* We pray that this book will be a blessing to you and to those whose lives you touch.

We express our love and admiration for you and recognize that you are beloved daughters of Heavenly Father and dedicated disciples of the Lord Jesus Christ. You are part of a great worldwide sisterhood. Guided by your motto, "Charity never faileth," you help strengthen families and build up the kingdom of God on the earth.

We encourage you to study this book and allow its timeless truths and inspiring examples to influence your lives.

We testify that the Lord has restored the fulness of the gospel through the Prophet Joseph Smith and that Relief Society is an important part of that restoration. Relief Society sisters have a glorious heritage. We pray that this volume will be an important resource for preserving that heritage.

The First Presidency

"Something Extraordinary"

Like Mary and Martha in the New Testament, Relief Society sisters today serve as faithful disciples of Jesus Christ.

In the first meeting of the Relief Society, Sister Emma Smith said, "We are going to do something extraordinary."[1] She was right. The history of Relief Society is filled with examples of ordinary women who have accomplished extraordinary things as they have exercised faith in Heavenly Father and Jesus Christ. Relief Society was established to help prepare daughters of God for the blessings of eternal life. The purposes of Relief Society are to increase faith and personal righteousness, strengthen families and homes, and provide relief by seeking out and helping those in need. Women fulfill these purposes as they seek, receive, and act on personal revelation in their callings and in their personal lives.

This book is not a chronological history, nor is it an attempt to provide a comprehensive view of all that the Relief Society has accomplished. Instead, it provides a historical view of the grand scope of the work of the Relief Society. Through historical accounts, personal experiences, scriptures, and words of latter-day prophets and Relief Society leaders, this book teaches about the responsibilities and opportunities Latter-day Saint women are given in Heavenly Father's plan of happiness.

Why Study the History and Work of Relief Society?

President Spencer W. Kimball, the twelfth President of the Church, said, "We know that women who have deep appreciation for the past will be concerned about shaping a righteous future."[2] A study of this book can help women increase their appreciation for the past and their understanding of their spiritual heritage.

The history of Relief Society teaches the divine identity and infinite worth of daughters of God. It is a Spirit-filled story of strong, faithful, purposeful women who have served with little public recognition. Through a study of this history, Latter-day Saints can see that

our Heavenly Father knows His daughters, that He loves them, that He trusts them with sacred responsibilities, and that He guides them as they fulfill those responsibilities. In their efforts, the women of the Church have united with men who hold the priesthood to build God's kingdom on the earth and strengthen the homes of Zion.

Personal study helps women learn their responsibilities in God's kingdom.

Personal Study of *Daughters in My Kingdom*

The value of this book is not so much in the dates and facts it provides but in the purposes, principles, and patterns it teaches. As individual Relief Society sisters study and refer to this book again and again, they will see that the heritage of Relief Society is not just about women who lived in the past; it is also about women all over the world today who make and keep covenants. This understanding can help sisters find inspiration from the past and feel peace as they face the future.

The teachings, stories, and examples in the book can guide sisters in establishing priorities and practices in their lives that will help them increase faith and personal righteousness, strengthen families and homes, and seek out and help those in need.

Sister Belle S. Spafford, the ninth Relief Society general president, said: "The average woman today, I believe, would do well to appraise her interests, evaluate the activities in which she is engaged, and then take steps to simplify her life, putting things of first importance first, placing emphasis where the rewards will be greatest and most enduring, and ridding herself of the less rewarding activities."[3]

As sisters learn from the history of Relief Society, they may discover examples, expressions, and principles that are especially meaningful to them. Inspired by these discoveries and by the teachings of ancient and latter-day prophets, they can seek, receive, and act on personal revelation. They can receive guidance as they strive to become the people the Lord wants them to become and do the things He would have them do.

Sisters can find encouragement in the words of Alma: "By small and simple things are great things brought to pass."[4] The small and simple things they accomplish will help them see how the Lord is strengthening them and guiding their lives.

Studying the History and Work of Relief Society with Others

This book is an important resource to help Relief Society sisters learn together on Sundays and on other days of the week. To find general instructions about teaching in Relief Society meetings, ward and branch Relief Society leaders can refer to the current handbook and to LDS.org. To find specific information about using this book in Relief Society meetings, they can visit LDS.org and refer to other supplemental instructions published by the Church.

The influence of this book is meant to extend beyond Relief Society meetings. Families may study and discuss the examples and teachings in the book together. Relief Society sisters

Sisters can edify one another as they discuss the history and work of Relief Society.

Appreciation is also expressed to the following: Susan W. Tanner, who was set apart in 2009 to write this first comprehensive history of Relief Society for the entire Church, using the work of Sister Tate and Sister Harris as a foundation; editors and designers, who captured the spirit of what this book could become and worked diligently to bring it about; other writers, contributors, and historians, who are recognized through citations of their published work in the notes at the end of this book.

Finally, this history never could have been written were it not for the faith, devotion, and service of Relief Society sisters throughout the history of the Church.

may share the book with their friends. Church members of all ages may use the book as a reference in lessons, talks, and council meetings.

Acknowledgments

Those who have prepared this book for publication express their gratitude to Lucile C. Tate and her niece Elaine R. Harris, who were called and set apart in 1996 to compile an unpublished history of the Relief Society. Their work was kept as a resource in the archives of the Church. Their effort to document the lives of Relief Society general presidents and the major events in Relief Society provided the foundation for this book.

Relief Society

A Restoration of an Ancient Pattern

Although the name may be of modern date, the institution is of ancient origin. We were told by our martyred prophet that the same organization existed in the church anciently.

Eliza R. Snow

Relief Society
A Restoration of an Ancient Pattern

Throughout His mortal ministry, the Savior showed special love and concern for women. Elder James E. Talmage of the Quorum of the Twelve Apostles said, "The world's greatest champion of woman and womanhood is Jesus the Christ."[1]

The Savior taught women in multitudes and as individuals, on the street and by the seashore, at the well and in their homes. He showed loving-kindness toward them and healed them and their family members. In many parables, He told stories of women engaged in ordinary activities. He demonstrated deep familiarity with women's lives and drew timeless gospel lessons from their everyday experiences. He forgave them. He wept with them. He had compassion on them in their specific circumstances as daughters, wives, homemakers, mothers, and widows. He appreciated them and ennobled them.

Even in excruciating pain on the cross, the Savior expressed concern for His mother, who by then was very likely a widow in need of watchcare.[2] And the first person to whom He appeared after His Resurrection was a woman.[3]

Female Disciples in the New Testament

While little is known about a formal organization of women in the New Testament, evidence suggests that women were vital participants in the Savior's ministry. The New Testament includes accounts of women, named and unnamed, who exercised faith in Jesus Christ, learned and lived His teachings, and testified of His ministry, miracles, and majesty. These women became exemplary disciples and important witnesses in the work of salvation.

Women journeyed with Jesus and His Twelve Apostles. They gave of their substance to assist in His ministry. After His death and Resurrection, women continued to be faithful disciples. They met and prayed together with the Apostles. They provided their homes as gathering places for Church members. They valiantly participated in the work of saving souls, temporally and spiritually.

Martha and her sister Mary are examples of female disciples in the New Testament. Luke 10 contains an account of Martha opening her home to Jesus. She served the Lord by taking care of His temporal needs, and Mary sat at the Master's feet and absorbed His teachings.

In an age when women were generally expected to provide only temporal service, the Savior taught Martha and Mary that women could also participate spiritually in His work. He invited them to become His disciples and partake of salvation, "that good part" that would never be taken from them.[4]

Mary and Martha became active participants in the Lord's mortal ministry. Later in the New Testament, we read Martha's strong testimony of the Savior's divinity. In a conversation with Jesus, she said, "I believe that thou art the

"Martha received [Jesus] into her house." Her sister Mary "sat at Jesus' feet, and heard his word" (Luke 10:38–39).

Christ, the Son of God, which should come into the world."[5]

Many other female disciples traveled with Jesus and the Twelve, learning from Him spiritually and serving Him temporally. Luke recorded:

"And it came to pass afterward, that he [Jesus] went throughout every city and village, preaching and shewing the glad tidings of the kingdom of God: and the twelve were with him,

"And certain women, which had been healed of evil spirits and infirmities, Mary called Magdalene, out of whom went seven devils,

"And Joanna the wife of Chuza Herod's steward, and Susanna, and many others, which ministered unto him of their substance."[6]

It is likely that these women provided some economic support for Jesus and His Apostles, along with service such as cooking. In addition to receiving Jesus's ministering—the glad tidings of His gospel and the blessings of His healing power—these women ministered to Him, imparting their substance and devotion.

The Apostle Paul wrote of women who, both in Church positions and of their own volition, served the Saints. His description of a righteous widow identified characteristics of many women in the early Church: "Well reported of for good works; if she have brought up children, if she have lodged strangers, if she have washed the saints' feet, if she have relieved

Throughout His mortal ministry, the Savior showed special love and concern for women.

"The cultivation of Christlike qualities is a demanding and relentless task—it is not for the seasonal worker or for those who will not stretch themselves, again and again."

Spencer W. Kimball
Ensign, *Nov. 1978*, 105

the afflicted, if she have diligently followed every good work."[7] Paul also wrote of the influence of wise, experienced older women. He counseled Titus to encourage older women to serve and teach young women about their eternal roles as wives and mothers, "that they may teach the young women to be sober, to love their husbands, to love their children."[8]

The book of Acts includes an account of a woman who embodied the virtues Paul described. Tabitha, who was also known as Dorcas, lived in Joppa, where she made clothes for women in need.

"Now there was at Joppa a certain disciple named Tabitha, which by interpretation is called Dorcas: this woman was full of good works and almsdeeds which she did.

"And it came to pass in those days, that she was sick, and died. . . .

"And forasmuch as [the city of] Lydda was nigh Joppa, and the disciples had heard that Peter was there, they sent unto him two men, desiring him that he would not delay to come to them.

"Then Peter arose and went with them. When he was come, . . . all the widows stood by him weeping, and shewing the coats and garments which Dorcas made, while she was with them.

"But Peter put them all forth, and kneeled down, and prayed; and turning him to the body said, Tabitha, arise. And she opened her eyes: and when she saw Peter, she sat up."[9]

The New Testament mentions other devoted women. Priscilla and her husband, Aquila, risked their lives for the Apostles and provided their home for Church gatherings.[10] Paul wrote, "Aquila and Priscilla salute you much in the Lord, with the church that is *in their house.*"[11]

A woman named Mary "bestowed much labour" for the Apostles.[12] A woman named Lydia was baptized along with her household and then ministered to those who had taught her.[13]

A woman named Phebe apparently held an ecclesiastical position of service in her congregation. Paul said, "I commend unto you Phebe our sister, which is *a servant of the church* . . . that ye receive her in the Lord, as becometh saints, and that ye assist her in whatsoever business she hath need of you: for she hath been *a succourer of many.*"[14] The kind of service rendered by Phebe and other great women of the New Testament continues today with members of the Relief Society—leaders, visiting teachers, mothers, and others—who act as succorers, or helpers, of many.

Tabitha *"was full of good works and almsdeeds"* (Acts 9:36).

Female Disciples in the Latter Days

The women in the ancient Church were dignified and noble, needed and valued. They served others, increased in personal holiness, and participated in the great work of saving souls.

These patterns have been restored in the latter days through the organization of the Relief Society. The Prophet Joseph Smith declared, "The Church was never perfectly organized until the women were thus organized."[15] Sister Eliza R. Snow, the second Relief Society general president, reiterated this teaching. She said: "Although the name may be of modern date, the institution is of ancient origin. We were told by our martyred prophet that the same organization existed in the church anciently."[16]

Besides Joseph Smith, other latter-day prophets have testified that the organization of Relief Society is an inspired part of the Restoration, whereby women in the Church are called in ecclesiastical positions to serve one another and to bless the entire Church. President Joseph F. Smith, the sixth President of the Church, said, "This organization is divinely made, divinely authorized, divinely instituted, divinely ordained of God to minister for the salvation of the souls of women and of men."[17] To a group of Relief Society sisters, President Lorenzo Snow, the fifth President of the Church, said: "You have ever been found at the side of the Priesthood, ready to strengthen their hands and to do your part in helping to advance the interests of the kingdom of God; and as you have shared in these labors, so you will most certainly share in the triumph of the work and in the exaltation and glory which the Lord will give to His faithful children."[18]

As women participate in Relief Society, they serve as valiant disciples of Jesus Christ in the work of salvation. Like the women in the ancient Church, they work alongside men who hold the priesthood to increase faith and personal righteousness, strengthen families and homes, and seek out and help those in need. Sister Julie B. Beck, the fifteenth Relief Society general president, taught: "Through Relief Society we practice being disciples of Christ. We learn what He would have us learn, we do what He would have us do, and we become what He would have us become."[19]

CHAPTER 2

"Something Better"

The Female Relief Society of Nauvoo

I now turn the key to you in the name

of God, and this society shall rejoice and

knowledge and intelligence shall flow

down from this time—this is the beginning

of better days to this society.

Joseph Smith

"Something Better"
The Female Relief Society of Nauvoo

In the spring of 1842, the Latter-day Saints in Nauvoo, Illinois, worked enthusiastically to build a temple in their city. The Prophet Joseph Smith encouraged everyone to help. Men did the actual construction of the temple, and women eagerly sought ways to contribute as well. Sarah M. Kimball recounted:

"The Nauvoo Temple walls were about three feet high. Strong appeals were being made by the President of the Church and others for help to forward the work.

"Miss [Margaret] Cook . . . one day in conversation with me on the subject of a recent appeal for provisions, clothing, bedding and general supplies for the workmen and their families, remarked that she would be pleased to contribute needlework if it could be made available. I proffered material for her to make up, and suggested that others might feel as we did. We then [discussed] the subject of organizing a sewing society. The object of which should be to aid in the erection of the temple.

"About a dozen of the neighboring sisters by invitation met in my [home] the following Thursday."[1]

In that era, it was a popular practice for women to form their own organizations, often with constitutions and bylaws—sets of rules to govern the organizations. The women who met at Sarah Kimball's home decided to establish a constitution and bylaws, and Eliza R. Snow accepted the responsibility to write them. Then the women asked Joseph Smith to review them and give his opinion of them. After the Prophet

The Saints felt an urgency to build the Nauvoo Temple.

read them, he said they were "the best he had ever seen. 'But,' he said, 'this is not what you want. Tell the sisters their offering is accepted of the Lord, and he has something better for them than a written constitution. I invite them all to meet with me and a few of the brethren . . . next Thursday afternoon, and I will organize the women under the priesthood after the pattern of the priesthood.' "[2]

Organizing the Relief Society

That next Thursday, on March 17, 1842, twenty women assembled on the upper floor of a building, often called "the red brick store," where Joseph Smith had an office and a business to support his family. They met under the direction of Joseph Smith and two members of the Quorum of the Twelve Apostles, Elders John Taylor and Willard Richards.[3]

Rather than pattern a Latter-day Saint women's organization after the women's societies that were prevalent and popular at that time, the Prophet Joseph Smith organized them in a divinely inspired and authorized manner.

Early in the meeting, he told the sisters that they were to encourage "the brethren to good works in looking to the wants of the poor—searching after objects of charity, and in administering to their wants—to assist by correcting the morals and strengthening the virtues of the female community."[4]

Joseph Smith's wife Emma was chosen to serve as the president of this new society. The

EMMA SMITH
First Relief Society General President

"I desire the Spirit of God to know and understand myself, that I might be able to overcome whatever of tradition or nature that would not tend to my exaltation in the eternal worlds. I desire a fruitful, active mind, that I may be able to comprehend the designs of God, when revealed through His servants without doubting."

Emma Smith

Letter to Joseph Smith, 1844, Church History Library

On March 17, 1842, Emma Smith became the first president of the Relief Society.

Prophet then encouraged his wife to choose counselors who, with her, would "preside over this society, in taking care of the poor—administering to their wants, and attending to the various affairs of this institution." Sister Smith chose Sarah M. Cleveland and Elizabeth Ann Whitney as her counselors. Elder Taylor later set apart each counselor by the laying on of hands to act in her office in the presidency.[5]

As the meeting continued, Joseph Smith said that his wife's calling fulfilled a prophecy revealed to him about 12 years earlier, in which the Lord spoke to her as "an elect lady, whom I have called" and told her that she would be "ordained under [Joseph Smith's] hand to expound scriptures, and to exhort the church, according as it shall be given thee by my Spirit."[6] Joseph Smith read

"The Relief Society was established by the spirit of inspiration, and has been guided by that spirit [ever since], and has instilled into the hearts of countless of our good sisters those desires for righteousness which have been pleasing to the Lord."

Joseph Fielding Smith

Relief Society Magazine, Dec. 1970, 883

that entire revelation, which is now section 25 of the Doctrine and Covenants, to those in attendance.[7]

In the revelation, the Lord told Emma of privileges that were to be hers, such as being a scribe for her husband and compiling hymns for the Saints. The Lord also counseled Emma to heed warnings, to be faithful and virtuous, to not murmur, to comfort her husband and be of help to him, to teach from the scriptures and exhort the Church, to write and learn, to "lay aside the things of this world, and seek for the things of a better," to keep covenants, to be meek and beware of pride, and to keep the commandments.[8]

At the conclusion of the revelation, the Lord declared that what He had said to Emma was not for her alone but was His "voice unto all."[9] With prophetic authority, Joseph Smith reiterated this point, emphasizing that the counsel and warnings in this revelation applied to all members of the newly organized society. He said "that not [Emma] alone, but others, may attain to the same blessings."[10] This revelation established foundational principles for Latter-day Saint women.

After some discussion, the sisters decided to call themselves the Female Relief Society of Nauvoo. Emma Smith declared: "We are going to do something extraordinary. . . . We expect extraordinary occasions and pressing calls."[11]

At the end of the meeting, Elder John Taylor shared his thoughts. He said that his "heart

John Taylor

rejoice[d]" when he saw "the most distinguished characters stepping forth in such a cause, which is calculated to bring into exercise every virtue and give scope to the benevolent feelings of the female heart." He also rejoiced "to see this institution organized according to the law of heaven—according to a revelation previously given to Mrs. [Emma] Smith appointing her to this important calling—and to see all things moving forward in such a glorious manner." His prayer was that "the blessings of God and the peace of heaven may rest on this institution henceforth." A choir then echoed Elder Taylor's remarks, singing "Come let us rejoice in the day of salvation" before the closing prayer.[12]

Priesthood Authority, Patterns, and Blessings

In a Relief Society meeting six weeks later, the Prophet Joseph Smith taught the sisters at length and then said: "This society is to get instruction through the order which God has established—through the medium of those appointed to lead—and I now turn the key to you in the name of God, and this society shall rejoice and knowledge and intelligence shall flow down from this time—this is the beginning of better days to this society."[13]

As the Lord's prophet, Joseph Smith held all the keys of priesthood authority on the earth. Therefore, when he organized the Relief Society to function under his overall direction, he unlocked opportunities for the women of the Church to play vital roles in the work of the Lord's kingdom. They now served under the authority of the priesthood and were promised blessings beyond those they had already received. These blessings would come to them

Through Peter, James, and John, the Lord bestowed "the keys of [His] kingdom" on Joseph Smith (see D&C 27:13).

according to their faithfulness and diligence. Knowledge and intelligence would flow to them as they received a fulness of priesthood blessings in the temple. They would receive ordinances and make sacred covenants that would help them prepare themselves and their families for eternal life. (For more on the Relief Society and the priesthood, see chapter 8.)

Early Excitement about Relief Society

The Female Relief Society of Nauvoo grew rapidly, reaching a membership of more than 1,100 in August 1842. Initially, membership in the society was not automatic for all female members of the Church. Women had to petition to belong, and they were accepted based on their goodness and virtue. Joseph Smith said, "There should be a select society, separate from all the evils of the world, choice, virtuous, and holy."[14]

Sisters in Nauvoo clamored to join the Relief Society. They were excited to give temporal and spiritual aid in an organized, authorized way. They also recognized the unparalleled opportunity to be taught by a prophet in preparation for higher spiritual knowledge and the blessings of the temple. They loved being unified with one another and with their priesthood brethren in these great causes.

Now that the sisters had this privilege, they had a responsibility to live up to it. Joseph Smith told them: "You are now placed in a situation where you can act according to those sympathies which God has planted in your bosoms. If you live up to these principles, how great and glorious!"[15] As President Boyd K. Packer of the Quorum of the Twelve Apostles said many years later, "It is as obligatory upon a woman to draw into her life the virtues that are fostered by the Relief Society as it is an obligation for the men to build into their lives the patterns of character fostered by the priesthood."[16]

Emma Smith conducted Relief Society meetings.

The Relief Society was not just another group of women trying to do good in the world. It was different. It was "something better" because it was organized under priesthood authority. Its organization was a necessary step in the unfolding of God's work on the earth. It prepared the women of the Church to receive priesthood ordinances and covenants, and it helped them with their family responsibilities.

Joseph Smith's Instructions

In the first meeting of the Female Relief Society of Nauvoo, Sister Eliza R. Snow was appointed to be the secretary of the organization. In that capacity, she took careful and detailed notes, which were called minutes, at each Relief Society meeting she attended. Joseph Smith told the sisters that these minutes would become the "constitution and law" of the society.[17]

In most Relief Society meetings, the sisters devoted time to receiving instruction. The sisters were blessed to be taught by the Prophet Joseph Smith in six of their meetings. As he taught, they felt rich outpourings of the Spirit. At the end of one of these meetings, Sister Snow recorded, "The Spirit of the Lord was poured out in a very powerful manner, never to be forgotten by those present on that interesting occasion."[18]

The Prophet Joseph Smith instructed Relief Society sisters.

Of all the minutes Sister Snow recorded, her notes of the Prophet's discourses were the most influential. The Prophet's teachings in this setting guided the work of the Relief Society sisters and the priesthood leaders who served with them. Those teachings continue to influence the work of the Church today.

Joseph Smith taught principles that helped Relief Society sisters "relieve the poor" and "save souls"—foundational principles upon which the society was built.[19] Established on this foundation, Relief Society has endured and increased in its influence. Since the early meetings of Relief Society, sisters have applied the Prophet's teachings in their efforts to increase faith and personal righteousness, strengthen families and homes, and seek out and help those in need.

Increase Faith and Personal Righteousness

Joseph Smith taught sisters that they had a solemn obligation to seek their own salvation. He said, "We can only live by worshipping our God—all must do it for themselves—none can do it for another."[20] He taught them to be righteous individuals, to become a holy people, and to prepare for temple ordinances and covenants. He encouraged them to be at peace with the Lord, with those around them, and with themselves: "Sisters . . . , shall there be strife among you? I will not have it—you must repent and get the love of God."[21] "Not war, not jangle, not contradiction, but meekness, love, purity, these are the things that should magnify us."[22]

In one Relief Society meeting, the Prophet Joseph discussed chapter 12 of the book of 1 Corinthians, emphasizing that each sister, fulfilling her own role, was important to the entire Church. He gave "instructions respecting the different offices [in the Church], and the necessity of every individual acting in the sphere allotted him or her; and filling the several offices to which they were appointed." He also warned against the disposition to "consider the lower offices in the Church dishonorable and to look with jealous eyes upon the standing of others." This, he said, "was the nonsense of the human heart, for a person to be aspiring to other stations than appointed of God."[23] Through such teachings, he helped the sisters walk "in holiness before the Lord."[24]

"If we would come before God," Joseph Smith told the Relief Society sisters, "let us be pure ourselves."[25]

Strengthen Families and Homes

Although the early Relief Society sisters were involved in their community and ready to serve their neighbors, they never lost sight of their responsibilities toward their own families and

"Bring up your children in light and truth" (D&C 93:40).

homes. They were true to their innate gifts as mothers and nurturers. They were also true to revelations the Lord had given through Joseph Smith about family responsibilities:

"The office of thy calling shall be for a comfort unto . . . thy husband, in his afflictions, with consoling words, in the spirit of meekness."[26]

"Inasmuch as parents have children in Zion, or in any of her stakes which are organized, that teach them not to understand the doctrine of repentance, faith in Christ the Son of the living God, and of baptism and the gift of the Holy Ghost by the laying on of the hands, when eight years old, the sin be upon the heads of the parents.

"For this shall be a law unto the inhabitants of Zion, or in any of her stakes which are organized.

"And their children shall be baptized for the remission of their sins when eight years old, and receive the laying on of the hands.

"And they shall also teach their children to pray, and to walk uprightly before the Lord."[27]

"I have commanded you to bring up your children in light and truth. . . .

". . . First set in order thy house. . . .

"What I say unto one I say unto all. . . .

". . . See that [family members] are more diligent and concerned at home, and pray always."[28]

Excerpts from the minutes of the Female Relief Society of Nauvoo indicate that Joseph Smith and the sisters never lost sight of the principles in these revelations. Their words and actions showed that their homes and the homes of others were uppermost in their minds. For example, Emma Smith taught that "it was high time for mothers to watch over their daughters and exhort them to keep the path of virtue."[29] The Prophet Joseph expressed special concern about the relationship between husband and wife. He counseled the sisters: "Let this society teach how to act towards husbands, to treat them with mildness and affection. When a man is borne down with trouble—when he is perplexed, if he can meet a smile, not an argument—if he can meet with mildness, it will calm down his soul and soothe his feelings. When the mind is going to despair, it needs a solace. . . . When you go home never give a cross word, but let kindness, charity and love, crown your works."[30]

"The future of the [Relief] Society is full of promise. As the Church grows, its field of usefulness will be correspondingly enlarged, and it will be even more potent for good than it has been in the past. If all the sisters will rally to the support of the society, it will accomplish a mighty work and be a continued blessing unto the Church."

Lorenzo Snow

Deseret Evening News, *July 9, 1901, 1*

In other settings, the Prophet gave similar counsel to men, saying that a husband's duty is to "love, cherish, and nourish his wife" and "regard her feelings with tenderness."[31]

When Relief Society sisters discussed ways to help people in their community, they often focused on families and homes. The minutes of their meetings are full of expressions such as the following: "Mrs. Hawkes spoke of the Drury family—still sick needing our prayers—if nothing more."[32] "Sister Joshua Smith . . . went and visited Sister McEwen and Sister Modley. Found them and their families in suffering want. They need attendance every day."[33] "P. M. Wheeler . . . would recommend to the charity of this society Sister Francis Lew Law, who is sick and without a home, an aged widow lady at present destitute of money."[34] "Sister Peck reported Mr. Guyes and family as sick and destitute. Administered to their relief. . . . Mrs. Kimball stated a Mr. Charleston and family were sick, his wife very low and in great need of a nurse. Said she had assisted them."[35]

The Saints' united effort to build a temple in Nauvoo was influenced by their love for their families. The Prophet Joseph had taught them that they could be baptized in behalf of their family members who had died. They were permitted to perform these ordinances outside a temple for a time, but the Lord had commanded them:

"Build a house to my name, for the Most High to dwell therein.

"For there is not a place found on earth that he may come to and restore again that which was lost unto you, or which he hath taken away, even the fulness of the priesthood.

"For a baptismal font there is not upon the earth, that they, my saints, may be baptized for those who are dead—

"For this ordinance belongeth to my house."[36]

They also wanted to build a temple so they could receive the new and everlasting covenant of marriage, by which their families could be united eternally.[37]

Church members in Nauvoo found great comfort in baptisms for the dead and the promise of eternal families. One of these

Baptismal font in the Helsinki Finland Temple

Preparing to Enter the Temple

Believe in Heavenly Father, Jesus Christ, and the Holy Ghost.

Cultivate a testimony of the Atonement of Jesus Christ and the restored gospel.

Sustain and follow the living prophet.

Qualify for a temple recommend by being morally clean, keeping the Word of Wisdom, paying a full tithing, and living in harmony with the teachings of the Church.

Give time, talents, and means to help build the Lord's kingdom.

Participate in family history work.

Be teachable and reverent.

Dress modestly and be well groomed.

members was a sister named Sally Randall. When her 14-year-old son George died, she sent the sad news to family members. Soon thereafter, she learned about baptism for the dead. Again she wrote to her relatives, this time with newfound peace and assurance:

"[George's] father has been baptized for him and what a glorious thing it is that we believe and receive the fulness of the gospel as it is preached now and can be baptized for all of our dead friends and save them as far back as we can get any knowledge of them. I want you [to] write me the given names of all of our connections that are dead as far back as grandfather's and grandmother's at any rate. I intend to do what I can to save my friends. . . . I expect you will think this is strange doctrine but you will find it to be true."

To her mother, who had also lost a child to death, Sally testified, "Oh, mother, if we are so happy as to have a part in the first resurrection, we shall have our children just as we laid them down in their graves."[38]

Provide Relief by Seeking Out and Helping Those in Need

Since the organization of the Church in 1830, Latter-day Saint women have found countless ways to give service. They have been true to the words of the Savior: "Inasmuch as ye have done it unto one of the least of these my brethren, ye have done it unto me."[39]

When the Prophet Joseph Smith led efforts to build a temple in Kirtland, Ohio, sisters saw many needs among the construction workers and their families. As Sarah M. Kimball recounted, "The women would churn and cheerfully send their butter to the workmen on the Temple and eat without any on their own tables."[40] The sisters also saw a need to make carpets and draperies for the temple. Polly Angell recalled a comment by Joseph

Smith as he saw them working. He said: "The sisters are always first and foremost in all good works. Mary [Magdalene] was first at the resurrection; and the sisters now are the first to work on the inside of the temple."[41]

With the Relief Society organized under priesthood authority, the effort to help those building the Nauvoo Temple was even greater. In one Relief Society meeting, the women concentrated on practical ways they could serve the men who were working so diligently on the temple. "The sisters expressed their feelings one by one," manifesting a unanimous "desire to assist in forwarding the temple and in aiding the cause of Zion." The minutes record many donations offered by Relief Society members:

"Sis. Jones said she would be willing to go about and solicit material, if counseled so to do—she also offered to board one to work on the temple.

"Mrs. Durfee said if the heads of the society wished, she is willing to go abroad with a wagon and collect wool etc. for the purpose of forwarding the work.

"Mrs. Smith suggested that merchant's wives donate material that others may be employed.

"Miss Wheeler said she is willing to give any portion, or all of her time—

"Mrs. Granger [is] willing to do anything, knit, sew, or wait on the sick, as might be most useful.

"Miss Ells said she had felt willing to go out and solicit donations etc.

"Mrs. Angell said she was willing to repair old clothes if necessary when new material cannot be obtained.

"Mrs. Smith proposed getting wool and furnish old ladies with yarn to knit socks to supply the workmen on the temple next winter.

"Sis. Stringham offered to make men's clothes and take work on the temple.

"Sis. Felshaw proposes to give some soap. . . .

"Sis. Stanley proposed giving every tenth pound of flax, also one quart milk per day.

"Miss Beman will make clothes.

"Sis. Smith proposed getting muslin etc. from merchants not belonging to the Church, who were friendly. . . .

"Sis. Geen offered to donate thread of her own spinning."[42]

From the hearts of these sisters flowed a great desire to engage in good works. They did so with wool and wagons, soap and sewing, food and finery, time and talents. Through their new society, the women of the Church acted according to their natural sympathies to build up the Lord's Church.

The Prophet Joseph Smith encouraged Relief Society sisters in their efforts to strengthen those in need. In one Relief Society meeting, after teaching them from 1 Corinthians 12 (see page 18), he began reading Paul's discourse on charity in 1 Corinthians 13. Commenting on this chapter, he said: "Don't be limited in your views with regard to your neighbors' virtues. . . . You must enlarge your souls toward others if you'd do like Jesus. . . . As you increase in innocence and virtue, as you increase in goodness, let your hearts expand—let them be enlarged towards others—you must be longsuffering and bear with the faults and errors of mankind. How precious are the souls of men!"[43]

In another Relief Society meeting, he taught: "Nothing is so much calculated to lead people to forsake sin as to take them by the hand and watch over them with tenderness.

When persons manifest the least kindness and love to me, O what power it has over my mind, while the opposite course has a tendency to harrow up all the harsh feelings and depress the human mind."[44]

Relief Society sisters embraced charitable service as a foundational principle of their organization. Each week as the Female Relief Society of Nauvoo met, individual sisters reported on people in need. A treasurer accepted donations, and the donations were dispersed to relieve the needy. Donations included money, supplies, talents, and time. Women gave articles of clothing and bedding.

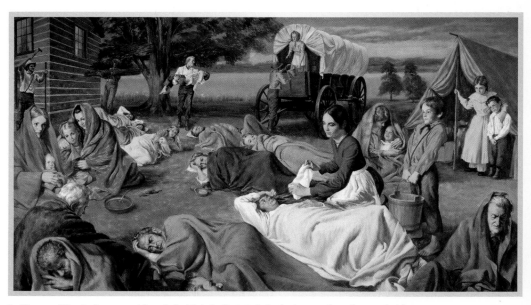

In Nauvoo, Illinois, Emma and Joseph Smith led efforts to help the hungry, homeless, and sick.

They offered flax, wool, and yarn that could be made into clothing. They also donated food: apples, onions, flour, sugar, bread, and butter.

Sister Emma Smith, as president of the Relief Society, was a paramount example of charitable service. She opened her home to the hungry, homeless, and sick. "The Homestead," as the Smiths' log home was sometimes called, consisted of a gathering room and two bedrooms. At the time of the organization of Relief Society, the home accommodated 11 people in addition to Emma, Joseph, and their 4 children.

Early Relief Society sisters served those in need and occasionally received service themselves. For example, Ellen Douglas joined the Relief Society soon after she and her family arrived in Nauvoo in March 1842. Three months later, her husband, George, died. She and her family worked together to provide for themselves, but they struggled without their husband and father. Still, Ellen participated in the work of the Relief Society by actively relieving others' suffering, sickness, and poverty. Then in April 1844, she and some of her children fell ill and found themselves in need of help. She wrote a letter to her family in England describing how the Relief Society came to her aid when she went to visit a friend named Ann:

"After I [had] begun to get well I went down into the city on a visit to where Ann lived, and I stayed two nights. . . . The woman where Ann lived would have me make application to the Female Relief Society for some clothing which I needed for myself and family. I refused to do so, but she said I needed something and that I had been so long sick and if I would not do it myself she would do it for me." Sister Douglas

JOSEPH SMITH
First President of the Church

"The [Relief] Society is not only to relieve the poor, but to save souls."

Relief Society Minute Book, June 9, 1842, Church History Library, 63

eventually agreed to ask for help. "We went to one of the sisters," she continued, "and she asked me what I needed most. I told her that I needed . . . many things. While I was sick my children [wore] out their clothes because I could not [mend] them, so she said she would do the best she could for me. Ann came over in a few days and they brought the wagon and fetched me such a present as I never received before."[45]

"That We May All Sit Down in Heaven Together"

Elder John A. Widtsoe of the Quorum of the Twelve Apostles described the foundational work of the Relief Society: "Relief of poverty, relief of illness; relief of doubt, relief of ignorance—relief of all that hinders the joy and progress of woman. What a magnificent commission!"[46]

Latter-day Saint women, strong in faith and testimony, have truly been given the "errand of angels."[47] Elder M. Russell Ballard of the Quorum of the Twelve Apostles taught: "Every sister in this Church who has made covenants with the Lord has a divine mandate to help save souls, to lead the women of the world, to strengthen the homes of Zion, and to build the kingdom of God."[48]

When Sarah M. Kimball and Margaret Cook decided to begin a sewing society, they wanted

Toronto Ontario Temple

to help prepare a temple for the people. Under the inspiration and guidance of a prophet and other priesthood leaders, they and their sisters ultimately helped prepare a people for the temple.

This work continues today. Guided by the principles Joseph Smith taught, Relief Society sisters work together to prepare women and their families for God's greatest blessings. They joyfully follow the counsel of Joseph Smith's mother, Lucy Mack Smith: "We must cherish one another, watch over one another, comfort one another and gain instruction, that we may all sit down in heaven together."[49]

"Cleave unto the Covenants"

Exodus, Migration, and Settlement

The sisters never lost sight of the institution, nor the promises made to them by President Joseph Smith. . . . They were always ready with willing hands and tender sympathies to perform deeds of love and charity, and many were in need of such kindly acts for those were the days of toil, and of suffering, of scarcity and of hardship.

Emmeline B. Wells

"Cleave unto the Covenants"
Exodus, Migration, and Settlement

On June 27, 1844, an armed mob advanced on a small jail in Carthage, Illinois, where Joseph Smith was imprisoned unjustly with his brother Hyrum and with Elders John Taylor and Willard Richards. When the mob left, Joseph and Hyrum were dead and Elder Taylor was wounded.

The martyrdom of Joseph and Hyrum Smith did not put an end to the Saints' faith and devotion. It also did not signal an end to the persecution of Church members. Because of continuing persecution, the Church's new leader, President Brigham Young, eventually counseled the Saints to leave Nauvoo, Illinois, for a new home, where they hoped to live and worship in peace. Many followed President Young, beginning their exodus in February 1846.

Leading up to this difficult time, the formal organization of the Female Relief Society was discontinued. However, the sisters' desires to relieve suffering, strengthen families, and be faithful and holy continued to burn bright. They followed the command the Lord had given their first Relief Society president: "Cleave unto the covenants which thou hast made."[1]

Exodus: Sustained by Covenants

The first Relief Society sisters were, like the ancient people of Ammon, "distinguished for their zeal towards God" and were "firm in the faith of Christ."[2] They had been taught by the Prophet Joseph Smith, and they had been blessed through their formal organization under the authority of the priesthood. Now they needed the blessings of the temple.

More than 5,000 Saints thronged the Nauvoo Temple after its dedication so they could receive the endowment and the sealing ordinance before embarking on their journey into an unknown future. They came to the temple all day and long into the night. President Brigham Young wrote that they were so anxious to receive their ordinances that "I have given myself up entirely to the work of the Lord in the Temple night and day, not taking more than four hours sleep, upon an average, per day, and going home but once a week."[3]

The strength, power, and blessings of temple covenants would sustain the Latter-day Saints during their journey, when they would suffer cold, heat, hunger, poverty, sickness, accidents, and death. They were strengthened and empowered—spiritually prepared to leave Nauvoo on their arduous journey into the wilderness.

Like many Relief Society sisters, Sarah Rich was buoyed by temple blessings as she faced the challenges of the exodus. Prior to leaving Nauvoo, she received a calling from Brigham Young to work in the temple. She later said:

"Many were the blessings we had received in the house of the Lord, which has caused us joy

Sarah Rich

and comfort in the midst of all our sorrows and enabled us to have faith in God, knowing He would guide us and sustain us in the unknown journey that lay before us. For if it had not been for the faith and knowledge that was bestowed upon us in that temple by the influence and help of the Spirit of the Lord, our journey would have been like one taking a leap in the dark. To start out . . . in the winter as it were and in our state of poverty, it would seem like walking into the jaws of death. But we had faith in our Heavenly Father, and we put our trust in Him feeling that we were His chosen people and had embraced His gospel, and instead of sorrow, we felt to rejoice that the day of our deliverance had come."[4]

As Sister Rich implied, the exodus was not a "leap in the dark" for faithful Latter-day

Saint women. They were sustained by their covenants. Like the children of Israel anciently, they followed a prophet into the wilderness in the hope of deliverance. In preparation for the exodus, President Brigham Young made the following declaration to the Saints: "This shall be our covenant—that we will walk in all the ordinances of the Lord."[5] Latter-day Saints walked into the wilderness bound by covenant to God, their families, and their fellow sojourners.

Migration: Faith, Charity, and Mutual Support

Before leaving Nauvoo, a group of Latter-day Saints wrote the following message on the wall of the assembly hall in their abandoned temple: "The Lord has beheld our sacrifice: come after us."[6] These words summarized their dedication and collective efforts. The Saints made the trek with a spirit of sacrifice, consecration, and faith in God. They did not make the journey as lone travelers but as the "Camp of Israel," a community organized into smaller groups, called companies, for mutual support.

In a revelation given to Brigham Young "concerning the Camp of Israel in their journeyings to the West," the Lord commanded the pioneers to "let each company bear an equal proportion, according to the dividend of their property, in taking the poor, the widows, the

More than 5,000 Saints received temple blessings in Nauvoo, Illinois, before embarking on their journey to the Salt Lake Valley.

"In any and every age of the world when God has called or commanded a man or a people to perform a certain work, they through determination and perseverance, and faith in him, have been enabled to accomplish it."

Wilford Woodruff

Deseret News: Semi-Weekly, July 26, 1881, 1

fatherless, and the families of those who have gone into the army."[7]

Often during the migration, the ratio of men to women and children was low. In the spring of 1847, after many Saints had spent the winter in a place they called Winter Quarters, about 520 men, accompanied by 35 women and 42 children, joined the Mormon Battalion to answer a call to serve in the United States military. Another 143 men, 3 women, and 2 children forged ahead in the first pioneer company, preparing the way for others. A sister named Presendia Kimball recalled: "Only a few men were left to raise grain and vegetables, and protect the women and children. . . . Thus were left the aged, the feeble, the women and the children."[8]

As the Saints traveled to the Salt Lake Valley, women helped one another take care of their families.

The Saints were blessed by priesthood power through the laying on of hands by brethren who held the priesthood. They were also sustained by the sisters' faith in God, charity, strength, and prayers.

With illness rampant, the sisters served as doctors and nurses to their own families and to one another, as they had in Nauvoo. Drusilla Dorris Hendricks recalled, "There was not a wagon in the whole camp, but what had sickness in it, [but] we bore it with the patience of Job."[9] The death rate was high, particularly among infants.[10]

Eliza Partridge Lyman gave birth to a son on July 14, 1846, in a wagon. Like many infants among the pioneers, the boy did not survive. In a journal, Eliza described her experiences:

July 14, 1846: "I am very uncomfortably situated for a sick woman. The scorching sun shining upon the wagon through the day and the cool air at night, is almost too much of a change to be healthy."

October 15, 1846: "We have taken possession of our log house today. The first house my babe was ever in. I feel extremely thankful for the privilege of sitting by a fire where the wind cannot blow it in every direction, and where I can warm one side without freezing the other. Our house is minus floor and many other comforts but the walls protect us from the wind if the sod roof does not from the rain."

December 6, 1846: "My baby [is] sick and getting worse. Has cried all day but I cannot see what ails him."

December 12, 1846: "The baby is dead and I mourn his loss. We have done the best we knew

Eliza Partridge Lyman

how for him, but nothing has done any good; he continued to fail from the time he was taken sick. My sister Caroline and I sat up every night with him and tried to save him from death, for we could not bear to part with him, but we were powerless. . . .

"I still have friends who are dear to me. If I had not I should wish to bid this world farewell, for it is full of disappointments and sorrow. But I believe there is a power that watches over us and does all things right." [11]

As Eliza said, she was sustained by the friendship of caring sisters. Later she provided that same friendship and compassion, helping other women who were dealing with similar grief. On June 1, 1847, she wrote: "Sister Elvira Holmes' babe died. Received an invitation . . . to come and spend the day with her which I accepted. Visited with her the grave of her child." [12]

In such trying circumstances, the sisters relied on the power of their covenants. Bathsheba W. Smith, the fourth Relief Society general president, later recalled those experiences:

"I will not try to describe how we traveled through storms of snow, wind, and rain; how roads had to be made, bridges built, and rafts constructed; how our poor animals had to drag on day after day with scanty feed; nor how our camps suffered from poverty, sickness, and death. We were consoled . . . by having our public and private meetings in peace, praying and singing the songs of Zion, and rejoicing

Many Latter-day Saint women gave birth to children during their journey to the Salt Lake Valley.

that we were leaving our persecutors far behind. We were further consoled by seeing the power of God manifested through the laying on of the hands of the elders, causing the sick to be healed, and the lame to walk. The Lord was with us and his power was made manifest daily." [13]

The women also found spiritual strength in each other's love and compassion. Throughout the journey, as they suffered trials of illness and death, they prayed in faith for each other and comforted each other. "The love of God flowed from heart to heart," wrote Helen Mar Whitney, "till the wicked one seemed powerless in his efforts to get between us and the Lord, and his cruel darts, in some instances, were shorn of their sting." [14]

Remembering inspired instruction from the Prophet Joseph Smith, these faithful pioneer women had a vision of their power and potential for service. They helped establish homes and communities. Through deeds of faith and charity, they saved souls. Their sacrifices had a sanctifying effect on themselves and on those who received their offerings.

Even without the formal meetings of the Relief Society, pioneer women followed prophetic teachings and kept their temple covenants, and in so doing they contributed to an extraordinary chapter in the history of the Church and the American West. A prominent non–Latter-day Saint historian wrote: "That I do not accept the faith that possessed them does not mean I doubt their frequent devotion

BATHSHEBA W. SMITH
Fourth Relief Society General President

"When I heard the Gospel I knew it was true; when I first read the Book of Mormon, I knew it was inspired of God; when I first beheld Joseph Smith I knew I stood face to face with a prophet of the living God, and I had no doubt in my mind about his authority."

Bathsheba W. Smith

Young Woman's Journal, *Oct. 1901, 440*

The sisters "were always ready with willing hands and tender sympathies to perform deeds of love" (Emmeline B. Wells).

and heroism in its service. Especially their women. Their women were incredible."[15]

Settlement: "Always Ready . . . to Perform Deeds of Love and Charity"

When the first pioneer companies arrived in the Salt Lake Valley, they planted crops and built shelters for their own survival. They also turned to meeting the needs of others. President Brigham Young counseled the Saints to assist those in need, both spiritually and temporally. His counsel was like Amulek's exhortation in the Book of Mormon to the impoverished

Zoramites: "If ye turn away the needy, and the naked, and visit not the sick and afflicted, and impart of your substance, if ye have, to those who stand in need—I say unto you, if ye do not any of these things, behold, your prayer is vain, and availeth you nothing, and ye are as hypocrites who do deny the faith."[16]

Sister Emmeline B. Wells, who later served as the fifth Relief Society general president, described the goodness and service of the sisters: "When the Saints left Nauvoo and during their journeyings, the Relief Society meetings were necessarily discontinued, though the sisters never lost sight of the institution, nor the promises made to them by President

In 1856, Relief Society sisters gathered quilts for suffering handcart pioneers.

charitable feelings of their hearts and gave service to meet the needs of those around them.

This pattern continued as more Latter-day Saints arrived in the Salt Lake Valley. Church leaders called people to settle the far reaches of the territory, expanding to areas north and south of Salt Lake City. Sisters remembered the legacy and foundational principles of the Female Relief Society of Nauvoo, and many groups were established in those settlements to serve others and relieve the poor.

Lucy Meserve Smith, for example, led a group of Latter-day Saint women in Provo, Utah. She and other sisters responded to calls to help Latter-day Saints who arrived in Utah. At the October 1856 general conference, President Brigham Young announced that handcart pioneers were stranded hundreds of miles away. He declared: "Your faith, religion, and profession of religion, will never save one soul of you in the celestial kingdom of our God, unless you carry out just such principles as I am now teaching you. Go and bring in those people now on the plains, and attend strictly to those things which we call temporal, or temporal duties, otherwise your faith will be in vain."[18]

Sister Smith recorded in her autobiography that after President Young's exhortation, those in attendance took action to provide relief for their brothers and sisters. Women "stripped

Joseph Smith, but continued their benevolent work wherever and whenever an opportunity presented itself; they were always ready with willing hands and tender sympathies to perform deeds of love and charity, and many were in need of such kindly acts for those were the days of toil, and of suffering, of scarcity and of hardship."[17]

In 1854, Matilda Dudley sensed many needs among local American Indians. Acting first on her own initiative and later on instruction from President Brigham Young, she organized sisters under the direction of her bishop to make clothing for native women and children. Similar groups developed in other settlements as Latter-day Saint women followed the off their petticoats [large underskirts that were part of the fashion of the day and that also provided warmth], stockings, and every thing they could spare, right there in the Tabernacle, and piled [them] into the wagons to send to the Saints in the mountains."

They continued to gather bedding and clothing for Saints who would arrive with only a few belongings in small handcarts. Sister Smith wrote: "We did all we could, with the aid of the good brethren and sisters, to comfort the needy as they came in with handcarts late in the fall. . . . As our society was short of funds then, we could not do much, but the four bishops could hardly carry the bedding and other clothing we got together the first time we met. We did not cease our exertions [un]til all were made comfortable." Sister Smith said that when the handcart companies arrived, a building in the town was "loaded with provisions for them." She continued: "I never took more satisfaction and, I might say, pleasure in any labor I ever performed in my life, such a unanimity of feeling prevailed. I only had to go into a store and make my wants known; if it was cloth, it was measured off without charge. [We] wallowed through the snow until our clothes were wet a foot high to get things together."[19]

"What Comes Next for Willing Hands to Do?"

These Relief Society sisters manifested charity, "the pure love of Christ,"[20] as they donated their petticoats and pieced quilts to save freezing, starving Saints whom they had never met. They found great joy in this service. After they had done all they could to help the handcart pioneers, they continued to help others. Lucy Meserve Smith's words expressed the feelings of their hearts: "What comes next for willing hands to do?"[21] This question epitomizes the goodness of Relief Society women—then and now. 🖉

Relief Society sisters continued to serve and encourage one another after they arrived in the Salt Lake Valley.

"A Wide and Extensive Sphere of Action"

If any of the daughters and mothers in Israel are feeling in the least [limited] in their present spheres, they will now find ample scope for every power and capability for doing good with which they are most liberally endowed. . . . President Young has turned the key to a wide and extensive sphere of action and usefulness.

Eliza R. Snow

CHAPTER 4

"A Wide and Extensive Sphere of Action"

On December 26, 1866, the First Presidency and Quorum of the Twelve Apostles met under the direction of President Brigham Young. Toward the end of the meeting, President Young, the second President of the Church, expressed a desire to reestablish Relief Societies throughout the Church.[1]

The following year, President Young felt increased urgency to assist bishops in their responsibility to seek out and help those in need. Initiating an effort to reestablish Relief Society in every ward, he shared the following counsel with bishops: "Let [the sisters] organize Female Relief Societies in the various wards. We have many talented women among us, and we wish their help in this matter. Some may think this is a trifling thing, but it is not; and you will find that the sisters will be the mainspring of the movement. Give them the benefit of your wisdom and experience, give them your influence, guide and direct them wisely and well, and they will find rooms for the poor and obtain the means for supporting them ten times quicker than even the Bishop could."[2]

Once again the sisters would be organized under the authority of the priesthood and, as the Prophet Joseph Smith had said, "placed in a situation where [they could] act according to those sympathies which God [had] planted in [their] bosoms."[3] They would strengthen their families and others in need, both temporally and spiritually. Through this service, their own faith and righteousness would increase. Sister

Construction of the Salt Lake Temple, 1877

Eliza R. Snow taught that the Relief Society would "refine and elevate [the sisters], and above all strengthen them in the faith of the Gospel, and in so doing, may be instrumental in saving many."[4]

A Relief Society in Each Ward

President Young called Sister Snow to serve the Church by traveling throughout the territory, helping bishops organize Relief Societies. She said, "President Young instructed the Bishops to organize Female Relief Societies in their various Wards, and . . . repeated the requisition, extending it to all the settlements, calling upon the sisters to enter into organizations, not only for the relief of the poor, but for the accomplishment of every good and noble work."[5]

As the secretary of the first Female Relief Society in Nauvoo, Illinois, Sister Snow had kept detailed minutes of the meetings, including the instructions from Joseph Smith (see chapter 2). On the trek from Nauvoo to the Salt Lake Valley, she had carefully safeguarded her minute book. She understood the importance of what had been taught to the sisters in those

ELIZA R. SNOW
Second Relief Society General President

"We like to be appreciated but if we do not get all the appreciation which we think is our due, what matters? We know the Lord has laid high responsibilities upon us, and there is not a wish or desire that the Lord has implanted in our hearts in righteousness but will be realized, and the greatest good we can do to ourselves and each other is to refine and cultivate ourselves in everything that is good and ennobling to qualify us for those responsibilities."

Relief Society Minute Book, 1868–79, Lehi Ward, Alpine Stake, Oct. 27, 1869, Church History Library, 27; punctuation and spelling modernized

Left to right: Elizabeth Ann Whitney, Emmeline B. Wells, and Eliza R. Snow

"This is what we desire to instill into the hearts of the sisters—to be useful in their sphere and not be discouraged because of difficulties in the way, but trust in God and look to Him, and His marvelous blessings, I will promise you, will be poured out upon you."

Lorenzo Snow

Young Woman's Journal, *Sept. 1895, 578*

meetings. She knew how the society should be structured, and she remembered the principles upon which it was established. She understood that the organization was a fundamental part of The Church of Jesus Christ of Latter-day Saints. "It is no ordinary thing," she explained, "to meet in an organization of this nature. This organization belongs to the organization of the Church of Christ, in all dispensations when it is in perfection."[6] Now, as she traveled from ward to ward, she taught from the minutes again and again.

Sister Eliza R. Snow instructed Relief Society sisters.

Expanding the Sisters' Vision and Influence

In addition to asking Sister Snow to work with priesthood leaders in each ward, President Young expanded her assignment. He said, "I want you to instruct the sisters."[7] Although she would not be set apart as the second Relief Society general president until 1880, she was given the same responsibilities the Lord had given Sister Emma Smith: "to expound scriptures, and to exhort the church, according as it shall be given thee by my Spirit."[8]

President Young also shared counsel with the women of the Church. His exhortations and

Sister Snow's teachings combined to expand the sisters' vision of their power for good in their families, in the Church, and in the world. Sister Snow said:

"If any of the daughters and mothers in Israel are feeling in the least [limited] in their present spheres, they will now find ample scope for every power and capability for doing good with which they are most liberally endowed. . . . President Young has turned the key to a wide and extensive sphere of action and usefulness."[9]

A review of some of the teachings and efforts that defined the Relief Society in the latter part of the 1800s shows how the reestablished Relief Society increased the vision and the righteous influence of Latter-day Saint women.

Charity

True to the pattern established by Joseph and Emma Smith in Nauvoo, charity continued to be the foundation of all things, both spiritual and temporal, that Relief Society sisters were organized to do. President Young taught:

"All this is embraced in our religion. Every good word and work, all things temporal, and all things spiritual, things in heaven, things on earth, and things that are under the earth are circumscribed by our religion. . . . If we do these things, and delight in doing right, our feet will be made [firm] and immovable like the bases of these everlasting hills. We ought not to desire anything [except] on righteous principles, and if we want right, let us then deal it out to others, being kind and full of love and charity to all."[10]

Turning from Worldly Influences

In his home, President Brigham Young taught his daughters to "retrench in everything that is bad and worthless, and improve in everything that is good and beautiful."[11] To retrench is to remove something. When President Young counseled his daughters to retrench, he meant for them to turn from worldly, frivolous, and immodest behavior and clothing. He also preached retrenchment and reform to the entire Church.

In counseling the Saints to forsake the ways of the world, President Young usually gave practical counsel that related to matters of daily living. He encouraged frugality and hard work. For example, he counseled the sisters in Relief Society to reform their eating and housekeeping patterns. But retrenchment meant more than adopting a simpler lifestyle; it meant a change of heart. Sisters were to set themselves apart from the rest of the world—truly becoming Saints, the Lord's people. Sister Eliza R. Snow said: "What do I want to retrench from? It is my ignorance and every thing that is not of God."[12]

Personal Revelation

Sister Snow followed the counsel of priesthood leaders, and she promised her sisters in the Relief Society that they would be blessed as they did the same. She also taught that individual women could receive inspiration to guide them in their personal lives, their families, and their Church responsibilities. She said: "Tell the sisters to go forth and discharge their duties, in humility and faithfulness and the Spirit of God will rest upon them and they will be blest in their labors. Let them seek for wisdom instead of power and they will have all the power they have wisdom to exercise."[13]

Her inspired instruction helped Relief Society sisters face the trials of their day. She taught that if they would continually seek guidance and comfort from the Holy Ghost, they could enjoy peace even in the midst of adversity. She said that the Holy Ghost "satisfies and fills up every longing of the human heart, and fills up every vacuum. When I am filled with that Spirit," she continued, "my soul is satisfied, and I can say in good earnest, that the trifling things of the day do not seem to stand in my way at all. But just let me lose my hold of that spirit and power of the Gospel, and partake of the spirit of the world, in the slightest degree,

As Relief Society sisters pray individually and with their families, they can receive inspiration to guide them.

and trouble comes; there is something wrong. I am tried, and what will comfort me? You cannot impart comfort to me that will satisfy the immortal mind, but that which comes from the Fountain above. And is it not our privilege to so live that we can have this constantly flowing into our souls?"[14]

Defending the Practice of Plural Marriage

In the early days of the Church, the practice of plural marriage was revealed to Joseph Smith.[15] Although this practice was initially difficult for many to accept, the faithful Saints knew that Joseph Smith was a prophet of God. They followed the Lord's will as it was revealed to their prophet. They made covenants with God and were strong and devout in keeping those covenants.

When the Relief Society was reestablished in the late 1860s, plural marriage was still part of Church members' lives. However, many people in the United States believed that women who lived the law of plural marriage were degraded and abused. As a result of a general misunderstanding about the Latter-day Saints and their beliefs, the national government passed legislation forbidding polygamous marriages.

A group of Latter-day Saint women gathered in Salt Lake City in January 1870 in response to this legislation. In the presence of newspaper reporters from across the United States, these women expressed their support for living prophets and for the practices of the Church. They defended themselves and their husbands and proclaimed their faith and their covenants. Sister Eliza R. Snow said: "It was high time [to] rise up in the dignity of our calling and speak for ourselves. . . . The world does not know us, and truth and justice to our brethren and to ourselves demands us to speak. . . . We are not inferior to the ladies of the world, and we do not want to appear so."[16]

One Latter-day Saint woman expressed the feelings of many others when she said: "There is no spot on this wide earth where kindness and affection are more bestowed upon woman, and her rights so sacredly defended as in Utah. We are here to express our love for each other, and to exhibit to the world our devotion to God our Heavenly Father; and to show our willingness to comply with the requirements of the Gospel; and the law of Celestial Marriage is one of its requirements that we are resolved to honor, teach, and practise, which may God grant us strength to do."[17]

Newspaper reporters said this was a "remarkable meeting."[18] One reporter wrote, "In logic and in rhetoric the so-called degraded ladies of Mormondom are quite equal to the . . . women of the East."[19] During the next few months, many more women participated in such meetings throughout the territory.

In 1890, President Wilford Woodruff, the fourth President of the Church, received a revelation that led to the Church's discontinuance of the practice of plural marriage. He wrote this revelation in a document known as the Manifesto. About writing the Manifesto, he said:

"Search the Scriptures—search the revelations which we publish, and ask your Heavenly Father, in the name of His Son Jesus Christ, to manifest the truth unto you, and if you do it with an eye single to His glory, nothing doubting, He will answer you by the power of His Holy Spirit. You will then know for yourselves and not for another. You will not then be dependent on man for the knowledge of God."

Joseph Smith
History of the Church, *1:282*

"The God of heaven commanded me to do what I did do; and when the hour came that I was commanded to do that, it was all clear to me. I went before the Lord, and I wrote what the Lord told me to write."[20]

Because the people had accepted the prophetic counsel to enter into plural marriages and had made and kept their covenants, this new revelation was once again difficult for many, but faithful Latter-day Saints determined again to follow the prophet. On the day that the general membership of the Church heard the Manifesto and approved it, Sister Zina D. H. Young, who was serving as the third Relief Society general president at the time, said, "Today the hearts of all were tried but looked to God and submitted."[21]

The women of the Church who, by revelation, embraced plural marriage and who, by revelation, later accepted the Manifesto are worthy of admiration and appreciation. They were strictly obedient to their covenants and the counsel of the living prophet. Today these women are honored by their faithful posterity.

A gathering of Latter-day Saint mothers and daughters, 1893

Helen Mar Whitney, who lived the law of plural marriage, wrote, "We may read the history of martyrs and mighty conquerors, and of many great and good men and women, but that of the noble women and fair daughters of Zion, whose faith in the promises of Israel's God enabled them to triumph over self and obey His higher law, and assist His servants to establish it upon the earth, . . . I feel sure there was kept by the angels an account of their works which will yet be found in the records of eternity, written in letters of gold." [22]

"Feast upon the words of Christ" (2 Nephi 32:3).

Articulating Beliefs

Sister Eliza R. Snow was a gifted writer and public speaker. She was known by many as "Zion's poetess" because of her skill with the English language.[23] She was knowledgeable, organized, faithful, untiring, unflinching, wise, and articulate, and she followed the promptings of the Spirit as she helped build the Lord's kingdom. She frequently shared her knowledge and her testimony, and she encouraged Latter-day Saint women to do the same in Relief Society meetings—not to depend on others to always teach them.

Some women felt reluctant and unprepared to speak in public. Sister Snow gave the following counsel to such sisters: "Do not let your president have to say all. . . . Has not God endowed you with the gift of speech? . . . If you are endowed with the Spirit of God, no matter how simple your thoughts may be, they will be edifying to those who hear you." [24]

Emily S. Richards said that Sister Snow helped her learn to speak in public: "The first time [she] asked me to speak in meeting, I could not, and she said, 'Never mind, but when you are asked to speak again, try and have something to say,' and I did." [25] Sister Richards continued to improve in her ability as a public speaker, and in 1889 she spoke at the National Woman Suffrage Association convention in Washington, D. C.

A journalist described Sister Richards as "trembling slightly under the gaze of the multitude, yet reserved, self possessed, dignified, and as pure and sweet as an angel. . . . It was not the words themselves but the gentle spirit [that] went with the words and carried winning grace to every heart."[26]

Today, Relief Society sisters follow the pattern set by Sister Snow, Sister Richards, and other early members of the Relief Society. They diligently seek gospel knowledge and then share that knowledge with others. In doing so, they follow the counsel of latter-day prophets. President Spencer W. Kimball, the twelfth President of the Church, said:

"I stress . . . the deep need each woman has to study the scriptures. We want our homes to be blessed with sister scriptorians—whether you are single or married, young or old, widowed or living in a family.

Spencer W. Kimball

"Regardless of your particular circumstances, as you become more and more familiar with the truths of the scriptures, you will be more and more effective in keeping the second great commandment, to love your neighbor as yourself. Become scholars of the scriptures—not to put others down, but to lift them up! After all, who has any greater need to 'treasure up' the truths of the gospel (on which they may call in their moments of need) than do women and mothers who do so much nurturing and teaching?"

President Kimball testified that Relief Society sisters will become a powerful influence for good upon the "good women of the world"

BRIGHAM YOUNG
Second President of the Church

"The sisters in our Female Relief Societies have done great good. Can you tell the amount of good that the mothers and daughters in Israel are capable of doing? No, it is impossible. And the good they will do will follow them to all eternity."

Deseret News Weekly, *June 16, 1869, 228*

as they "reflect righteousness and articulateness in their lives."[27]

Sister Snow, President Kimball, and many other Church leaders have shared a vision of Relief Society's influence for good. As sisters articulate their beliefs by word and deed, they can strengthen each other's faith in Heavenly Father and Jesus Christ. They can help each other prepare to receive all the blessings available in Heavenly Father's plan of happiness.

Temporal Self-Reliance

The Latter-day Saints gathered in the Salt Lake Valley after having been persecuted and forced from their homes and communities multiple times. Now that they had migrated to a faraway and isolated desert, President Brigham Young wanted them to flourish and establish a permanent home for themselves. He wanted them to be safe from physical harm, and he also wanted them to keep themselves safe from worldly influences that could harm their faith and their testimonies. He wanted them to be independent from worldly influences, both temporally and spiritually.

This meant that the Saints needed to learn skills that would allow them to take care of all their needs. In this effort, President Young had great trust in the capacities, talents, faithfulness, and willingness of the women. He reminded Relief Society sisters to fulfill their duties at

Becoming Self-Reliant

Learn to love work and avoid idleness.

Acquire a spirit of self-sacrifice.

Accept personal responsibility for spiritual strength.

Accept personal responsibility for health, education, employment, finances, food, and other life-sustaining necessities.

Pray for faith and courage to meet challenges that come.

Strengthen others who need assistance.

home with their husbands and children.[28] He also taught other duties of temporal self-reliance, some of which are mentioned below. While many specific temporal duties are different today, the principles behind these duties remain constant: Latter-day Saints are counseled to do all they can to provide the temporal necessities of life for themselves and their families.

Sewing. President Young advised sisters to sew clothes for themselves and their families. He said, "I call upon my sisters to . . . create your own fashions, and make your clothing to please yourselves independent of outside influences."[29] Sister Eliza R. Snow reported that he encouraged sisters to establish "fashions that would be becoming—such as would be worthy the patronage of sensible, refined and intelligent women who stand, as we in reality do, at the head of the world."[30]

Silk. President Young established the Deseret Silk Association, with Zina D. H. Young as its president. This group raised silkworms, feeding them mulberry leaves. Sister Young abhorred the worms and even suffered nightmares about them, but she obediently hatched and raised them in her own cocoonery and taught others to do the same. Under her direction, the Deseret Silk Association raised silkworms for over 20 years. Although their work never provided income, they were able to spin lovely silk for themselves.

Wheat. President Young counseled the sisters, "Learn to sustain yourselves; lay up grain and flour, and save it against a day of scarcity."[31] Emmeline B. Wells, who later became the fifth Relief Society general president, was assigned to be in charge of the central wheat committee.

Early Relief Society sisters harvesting silk, about 1890

In this venture, the women were motivated by their motherly desire to protect their families from hunger. Sister Wells said: "Who is there that can feel these things as deeply as a mother can? Think what it would be to hear your little one cry for bread."[32]

Ward Relief Society presidents met periodically to discuss ways to procure and store the grain. The willing expression of Sarah Howard, a ward Relief Society president in Salt Lake City, represented the sentiments of many sisters at the time. She said: "I feel it is a privilege the Lord has given us, and we will try and be united in it. For my part I will try and do all I can, and I feel that the Lord will open a way whereby we can obtain grain, although it is late in the season."[33] Sarah M. Kimball, who also served as a ward Relief Society president, already had a storage plan in mind when she came to one meeting. In the first year of the project, her ward Relief Society built a fireproof granary with a capacity to store 1,000 bushels of wheat.

President John Taylor of the Quorum of the Twelve Apostles encouraged brethren in Kaysville, Utah, to help the sisters in this effort. He told of a woman who felt that her husband was "a little too liberal and careless" with the family's finances. Each week she slipped part of her household budget into the family Bible. "Some years afterwards there came a financial crisis, and [the] husband was troubled. The wife readily perceived the change in her husband's countenance, and she asked him to tell her the cause of his trouble. He told her that he had a [bill] coming due, and he was afraid he could not meet it. She tried to encourage him by telling him

"By the power of the living God we can and we will be self-sustaining and be the most independent creatures under the celestial world."

Harold B. Lee
Church News, *Feb. 12, 1944, 8*

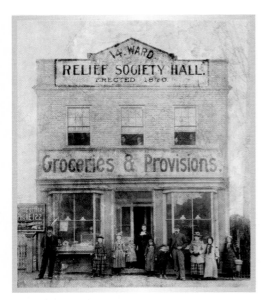

A Relief Society meeting hall, on the floor above a grocery store in Salt Lake City, Utah, 1892

of emergency."[35] This was fulfilled in 1898 and 1899, when Relief Society wheat provided sustenance during a severe drought in southern Utah.

The sisters' diligence in preserving wheat allowed Latter-day Saint women to serve people beyond their families and fellow Saints. The Church sent Relief Society wheat to American Indians in Utah; to survivors of a terrible earthquake and fire in San Francisco, California, in 1906; and to people in China who were suffering from a famine in 1907.[36] The wheat also provided nourishment for thousands during World War I, when the Relief Society sold 200,000 bushels to the United States government.[37] This legacy of preservation and service helped establish a pattern for the Church's present efforts to give humanitarian aid throughout the world, wherever people are in need.

Health care and medical education. In September 1873, Sister Eliza R. Snow reported that President Brigham Young wanted "a good many [sisters] to get a classical education, and then get a degree for Medicine."[38]

Sister Zina D. H. Young serves as an example of a Relief Society sister who gave great service in the medical field. She was told in her patriarchal blessing that she had the gift to heal, and she prepared herself to take advantage of this gift by taking a course in obstetrics—the medical

to have faith in God, and referred to the good, old Book, telling him to read it, that he might get some comfort from it. She handed him the Bible, and as he opened it and turned over the leaves the [money] began to drop out." President Taylor concluded, "We may find a time when we may need this wheat that our sisters are storing up; let us not be too confident about our affairs, and do what we can by way of helping them."[34]

Sister Emmeline B. Wells told the sisters that their diligence in this effort would be "the temporal salvation of this people in case practice dealing with the birth of children. She helped deliver many babies in the Salt Lake Valley. In her service, her practical education complemented her gifts to nurture physically, heal spiritually, and comfort emotionally. Sister Emmeline B. Wells said of her: "Numberless instances might be cited of her ministrations among the sick, when she seemed to be inspired by some higher power than her own . . . when courage and faith had failed in those around the sickbed. At such times she seemed an angel of mercy in very deed."[39]

Despite all the service Sister Young gave as she relied on her spiritual gifts and limited

LDS Hospital nursing graduates, class of 1911

education, she was acutely aware that she could not meet all the medical needs of the growing population in Utah. She encouraged other Latter-day Saint women to follow President Young's counsel to receive medical training.

Sister Snow said: "Are there here, now, any sisters who have ambition enough, and who realize the necessity of it, for Zion's sake, to take up this study? There are some who are naturally inclined to be nurses; and such ones would do well to study Medicine. . . . If they cannot meet their own expenses, we have means of doing so."[40]

With this encouragement, some Relief Society sisters studied medicine in the eastern United States. They came back to Utah as doctors and taught classes in midwifery and home nursing. Emma Andersen Liljenquist, who attended the classes in Utah, recorded some of her experiences:

"I enjoyed [the course] very much, and after being set apart by Apostle John Henry Smith and several of the others, I returned home to do my work, having been promised by the Apostles that if I lived right I should always know what to do in case of any difficulties. . . .

"That promise has been fulfilled to the very letter. Many times when one of my patients was seriously ill, I have asked my Heavenly Father for assistance, and in every case it was given to me. One in particular was a lady who had just given birth to a baby and hemorrhage set in. The husband called the doctor, but he did not realize that it was so serious. I . . . asked the Lord to help us. The hemorrhage ceased and I did the necessary things for her. When the doctor arrived, he said he could hardly believe what had happened, but said I had done exactly what he would have done. . . .

". . . I have brought over one thousand babies [into the world]. Once again I give thanks to my Heavenly Father for His help and the strength the Lord has given me, for without it I could not have rendered this service to my sisters or our community. One of the most touching things about a birth is that the mother's first concern is about her baby, not herself." [41]

In 1882 the Relief Society established the Deseret Hospital, "where the sick of the Lord's people could be attended and have the benefit of the ordinances of the Church [priesthood blessings] as well as skilful treatment." [42] The hospital continued for a little more than a decade until its operating costs exceeded the donations given and other facilities became available.

ZINA D. H. YOUNG
Third Relief Society General President

"I rejoice in putting my testimony before the daughters of Zion, that their faith may be strengthened, and that the good work may roll on. Seek for a testimony, as you would, my dear sisters, for a diamond concealed. If someone told you by digging long enough in a certain spot you would find a diamond of unmeasured wealth, do you think you would begrudge time or strength, or means spent to obtain that treasure? . . . If you will dig in the depths of your own hearts you will find, with the aid of the Spirit of the Lord, the pearl of great price, the testimony of the truth of this work."

Zina D Young

Young Woman's Journal, *Apr. 1893, 319*

Women's Suffrage (the Right to Vote)

In February 1870 the territorial government of Utah granted women the right to vote in government elections. At that time, the territory of Wyoming was the only other place in the United States where women were given this right. Later the national government rescinded this privilege as part of the punishment for Latter-day Saints living the law of plural marriage. But Latter-day Saint women remained vocal and articulate about their rights. Many sisters actively sought women's suffrage, or the right to vote. Their increasing ability to speak articulately was a blessing when they needed to represent themselves as strong, dignified, and ennobled women. Through their efforts, they regained the right to vote when Utah was granted statehood in the United States of America. They also gained the respect of other women's movements in the United States and around the world.

Publications

Under Sister Eliza R. Snow's leadership, the Relief Society supported a newspaper titled the *Woman's Exponent.* This newspaper was written for Latter-day Saint women to help them learn about their work, their lives, and their history. Sister Emmeline B. Wells served as the editor during most of the newspaper's publication. In her diary she wrote, "I desire to do all in my power to help elevate the condition of my own people, especially women."[43] She later wrote, "I have desired with all my heart to do those things that would advance women in moral and spiritual as well as educational work and tend to the rolling on of the work of God upon the earth."[44]

After 42 years of publication, the *Woman's Exponent* was discontinued in 1914. The next year, the Relief Society began publishing the *Relief Society Magazine,* which included lessons for weekly Relief Society meetings. The magazine was an important resource for sisters. Women treasured their copies, learning from

The Woman's Exponent, *a newspaper for Relief Society sisters, was published from 1872 to 1914.*

them and teaching from them. In 1971, the *Relief Society Magazine* and other magazines for English-speaking adult members of the Church were merged into one magazine, called the *Ensign.* Since that time, the *Ensign* has provided articles to instruct and inspire Relief Society sisters.

The Church began publishing magazines in languages other than English in the mid-1800s. Many of these magazines were published under the direction of mission presidents. In 1967 they were unified into one magazine with the same format and content, translated into many different languages. This international magazine—now called the *Liahona*—has always provided articles to help sisters live the gospel.

Since 1987, visiting teaching messages have been published in the *Liahona* and the *Ensign.* Visiting teaching messages are also distributed as separate publications in areas where the Church is new and membership is limited.

Preparing Children and Young Women for Service in God's Kingdom

In the late 1800s, priesthood and Relief Society leaders organized efforts to improve the lives of children and young women. Acting on President Brigham Young's call to reform and retrench (see page 45), Relief Society leaders established the Young Ladies Department of their Cooperative Junior and Senior Retrenchment Association in 1870. This led to today's Young Women organization. The Primary was organized for children in 1878. Initially, Relief Society leaders supervised the work of these organizations under the direction of priesthood leaders. In 1880, President John Taylor, the third President of the Church, extended callings to a general Relief Society presidency, a general Young Women presidency, and a general Primary presidency, differentiating the work of these three organizations.

Since then, Relief Society sisters have always led and served in the Young Women and Primary organizations. They have also strengthened the rising generation through service in other organizations, such as Sunday School and seminaries and institutes.

Moving Forward

The reestablishment of the Relief Society led to greater responsibilities and greater opportunities for Latter-day Saint women. Eliza R. Snow declared:

"Don't you see that our sphere is increasing? Our sphere of action will continually widen, and no woman in Zion need[s] to mourn because her sphere is too narrow.

"God bless you, my sisters, and encourage you, that you may be filled with light, and realize that you have no interests but in the welfare

"I will go forward. . . . The 'testimony of Jesus' will . . . guide my vision" (Eliza R. Snow).

Sister Snow's personal expression of faith and optimism can serve as a guide for all Latter-day Saints. "I will go forward," she said. "I will smile at the rage of the tempest, and ride fearlessly and triumphantly across the boisterous ocean of circumstance . . . and the *'testimony of Jesus'* will light up a lamp that will guide my vision through the portals of immortality."[46]

of Zion. Let your first business be to perform your duties at home. But, inasmuch as you are wise stewards, you will find time for social duties, because these are incumbent upon us as daughters and mothers in Zion. By seeking to perform every duty you will find that your capacity will increase, and you will be astonished at what you can accomplish."[45]

"Charity Never Faileth"

Charity suffereth long, and is kind,

and envieth not, and is not puffed up,

seeketh not her own, is not easily provoked,

thinketh no evil, and rejoiceth not in

iniquity but rejoiceth in the truth, beareth

all things, believeth all things, hopeth all

things, endureth all things.

Moroni 7:45

"Charity Never Faileth"

When Sister Emmeline B. Wells was called in 1910 to serve as the fifth Relief Society general president, she was prepared for the responsibility. As a participant in the migration to the Salt Lake Valley, she had worked side by side with sisters who had abiding testimonies of the gospel of Jesus Christ and who understood the foundational principles of Relief Society. She had served as secretary to two general Relief Society presidents, Zina D. H. Young and Bathsheba W. Smith, from 1888 to 1910.

With a testimony that the Relief Society had been organized by revelation, Sister Wells and her counselors, Clarissa S. Williams and Julina L. Smith, were committed to preserving the principles upon which the society had been founded. In October 1913 they said:

"We do declare it our purpose to keep intact the original name and initial spirit and purpose of this great organization, holding fast to the inspired teachings of the Prophet Joseph Smith when he revealed the plan by which women were to be empowered through the calling of the priesthood to be grouped into suitable organizations for the purpose of ministering to the sick, assisting the needy, comforting the aged, warning the unwary, and succoring the orphans."[1]

A few months earlier, this sense of purpose had led Sister Wells and her counselors to establish a motto that would become a constant reminder of the organization's founding principles and inspired origins. They chose a scriptural declaration: "Charity never faileth."[2] These three words embraced the charge that the Prophet Joseph Smith had given the Relief Society sisters: to "relieve the poor" and to "save souls."[3]

In the past, pioneer women had practiced charity for close neighbors. Now Relief Society sisters would organize themselves to extend charity, "the pure love of Christ,"[4] to worldwide neighbors as well.

Sister Wells and her counselors established this motto in a time of relative peace and prosperity. Little did they know how events in the coming years would put their motto to the test.

Living Peaceably in a Time of War

War broke out in Europe in 1914. By the time the war ended in November 1918, many nations had joined the conflict, which came to be known as World War I. During this period, when bitterness and intolerance could have threatened the charitable feelings expected from Relief Society sisters, Sister Emmeline B. Wells and her counselors issued the following message to all women in the Church:

"Administer in the spirit of love and patience to your husbands and to your children; guard the little ones; do not permit them to imbibe the spirit of intolerance or hatred to any nation or to any people; keep firearms out of their hands; do not allow them to play at war nor to find amusement in imitating death in battle; inculcate the spirit of loyalty to country and flag, but help them to feel that they are soldiers of the Cross and that if they must needs take up arms in the defense of liberty, of country and homes they shall do so without rancor or bitterness. . . . Teach the peaceable things of the kingdom [and] look after the needy more diligently than ever."[5]

In sending this message, Sister Wells urged sisters to put charity into action, just as the Prophet Joseph Smith had taught over 70 years earlier. She encouraged them to be patient with loved ones and kind toward neighbors—including enemies—and to give service to those in need. Relief Society sisters followed this counsel. They sought to receive and share the pure love of Christ, which they knew would

EMMELINE B. WELLS
Fifth Relief Society General President

"It is [my] strongest desire that our young women of today be made to comprehend the work of the early members who, without the facilities of the present time, comforted the sad and distressed, visited the widow and fatherless, and were like ministering angels."

Emmeline B. Wells

Relief Society Bulletin, May 1914, 3

Relief Society sisters preparing layettes (sets of baby clothes) for families in need

never fail them.[6] This love would sustain them through seasons of war and peace.

During World War I, the Relief Society in the United States cooperated wholeheartedly with community organizations such as the National Council of Defense and the American Red Cross. The sisters participated in food production and conservation, fund drives, sanitation, child welfare work, and other service. They were effective and energetic in cooperating with these community efforts. However, their prophet reminded them that they must never lose sight of the divine origins of Relief Society.

President Joseph F. Smith, the sixth President of the Church, said that while worldly organizations "are men-made, or women-made," the Relief Society "is divinely made, divinely authorized, divinely instituted, divinely ordained of God to minister

Joseph F. Smith

for the salvation of the souls of women and of men." He did not want "to see the time when our Relief Societies will follow, or commingle and lose their own identity by mixing up with these woman-made organizations that are coming to pass. . . . It is for you," he told Relief Society sisters, "to lead the world and to lead especially the women of the world, in everything that is praise-worthy, everything that is God-like, everything that is uplifting and that is purifying to the children of men. You are the head, not the tail."[7] Sister Emmeline B. Wells shared this vision. She guided the Relief Society in cooperating with other organizations, but she also helped maintain the society's distinctive purpose and divine nature.

In addition to working with other organizations, Relief Society sisters did a variety of things on their own and with their wards to provide goods and raise money for those in need. Some sisters made and sold dresses, aprons, children's clothing, quilts, and handwoven hats and rugs. Some raised and sold cattle and sheep.

A sister in Tooele, Utah, learned that a quilt she made had offered relief to a British family during the war. This Relief Society sister had made the quilt in 1906, tucked a note inside it, and sent it

to San Francisco, California, to help victims of a terrible earthquake. Eleven years later, the quilt was given to the Red Cross and sent to Great Britain. When the British recipient found the note, she sent a personal thank-you letter, saying that the quilt "came in very useful, as I lost my husband at the front." Left with eight children and no possibility of working, this widow admitted, "It is as much as I can do to keep going."[8]

Many British sisters volunteered to sew and knit for the soldiers, but they had no money to buy the materials they needed. American and Canadian Relief Societies eagerly contributed to an emergency fund to help. They sent money to each branch in Great Britain so the British sisters could buy material for making sheets, pillowcases, and clothing.

When the Relief Society sold its remaining wheat to the United States government in 1918 (see chapter 4), Sister Wells observed, "In all these years we have not had much need to use the grain stored away for the purpose it was designed, but with the dark cloud hovering over the world as it now does, we can see the prophetic wisdom of President Young in calling upon the sisters to save grain against a time of need."[9]

The wheat sale did more than provide food for people who were hungry. Sister Clarissa S. Williams, who served as one of Sister Wells's counselors in the presidency, recommended that the Relief Society preserve the funds from the sale in a central account and that they use the interest to finance efforts to improve the health of women and children. Later, when Sister Williams served as the sixth Relief Society general president, she oversaw the use of those funds for such purposes.

Strengthening Individuals and Families

At the end of World War I, many families and individuals were in need—financially, physically, emotionally, and spiritually. To meet these needs, the Relief Society established the Relief Society Social Service Department in 1919, with the full support of President Heber J. Grant, the seventh President of the Church. Sister Amy Brown Lyman, who later became the eighth Relief Society general president, served as the director of the department. Through the Social Service Department, the Relief Society cooperated with wards and stakes in efforts such as helping needy women and girls find employment and placing children for adoption. Its primary purpose, however, was to provide practical training for families. Sister Lyman said

Relief Society sisters in Kidderminster, England

that the Relief Society Social Service Department was not a "relief-giving agency" but a "service department," emphasizing "the study of family situations, the making of plans and budgets, the organizing of relief where LDS families [are] concerned, and the training of workers."[10]

With this goal in mind, the Social Service Department created a six-week training program in family welfare. Stake workers took this class and then went back to their wards and communities and taught it. Over 4,000 women were trained.

Beginning in 1902, the Relief Society general presidency had sponsored a program for training nurses. By 1920, professional training for nurses had become more extensive, so the Relief Society established a training program for nurses' aides. This one-year course, which began at LDS Hospital in Salt Lake City, Utah, did not charge tuition. Instead, the students were required to give 30 days of free nursing service in their communities. After 4 years, in which 46 aides were trained, the Relief Society discontinued the program and transferred their support to Red Cross home-nursing courses.

Nurses and children enjoying music at LDS Hospital in Salt Lake City, Utah, 1934

As with some other programs, the Relief Society used this program to meet a specific temporal need of the time and then turned the work over to other agencies.

Relief Society leaders encouraged sisters to continue serving one another in charitable ways, as they had done from the beginning days in Nauvoo. Sisters cared for the sick, sewed for those who needed clothing, and gave relief in other ways to those in need. For example, in 1921 a group of Armenian Latter-day Saints living in Turkey had to evacuate their homes. Joseph W. Booth, the president of the Palestine-Syrian Mission, helped them move to Aleppo, Syria, where he organized a branch with a Relief Society of about 30 sisters. Most of these women were very poor, and yet they felt it was their privilege and duty as Relief Society women to serve those who were less fortunate than they. So they gathered together and sewed clothing from 100 yards of cloth that President Booth had purchased. They also prepared a meal for undernourished fellow refugees.

In April 1921, Sister Clarissa S. Williams succeeded Sister Emmeline B. Wells as Relief Society general president. Having served in the presidency with Sister Wells, she was ready for the challenges that would come. She was known for her organizational skills and her love and friendship to all.

Joseph W. Booth and Relief Society sisters from Armenia in the early 1920s

Sister Williams was concerned about the high mortality rate of mothers and infants. She was also concerned about the lack of opportunities for the disabled and the low standard of living for many women. Under her wise and able leadership, Relief Societies continued their efforts to alleviate these problems. In 1924, with support and encouragement from general and local priesthood leaders and Sister Williams, the Cottonwood Stake Relief Society established a maternity hospital. This hospital later became part of a network of Church hospitals.

Sister Williams saw a great need for advancement in "health, opportunity, and a decent standard of living for all those with whom we come in contact." She said, "Such an undertaking for general betterment comprehends careful preparation, training, educational work, and actual service."[11] These efforts helped meet present demands, giving bishops an avenue for providing assistance for needy families. They also prepared the Church to respond to difficulties that would come a few years later.

Cultivating Self-Reliance

For more than a decade after World War I, the Relief Society worked to improve the standard of living for women and families, focusing on health, jobs, and education. The Relief Society also continued to encourage personal

righteousness and acts of charity. Then, with little warning, the world plunged into a great economic depression at the end of 1929.

Once again the qualities taught and learned in Relief Society strengthened individuals and families in a time of crisis. Latter-day Saint women found strength in their faith in Heavenly Father and Jesus Christ, drew on their skills of self-reliance, and worked to express the charity in their hearts. With these principles to guide them, they were able to take care of themselves and their families while reaching out to others.

In 1928, President Heber J. Grant called Sister Louise Y. Robison to serve as the seventh Relief Society general president. Economic challenges were not new to Sister Robison. She had grown up in a humble log home in

LOUISE Y. ROBISON
Seventh Relief Society General President

"If we only half do our work we will have no pleasure, if we do it from a sense of duty we will have no joy, but if we feel we are a branch of this vine, and that our Father in Heaven has felt us to be worthy to be a member of that branch, and that we can carry this work when it is here to do, then we will have joy."

Louise Y. Robison

Relief Society Magazine, *Nov. 1933, 649*

rural Scipio, Utah, where she had learned to farm, garden, sew, work hard, live on little, and be of good cheer.

Seven years before calling Sister Robison to be Relief Society general president, President Grant had set her apart to serve as second counselor in the general Relief Society presidency. She had felt her inadequacies keenly, as her daughter recounted:

"When Mother went to President Grant's office to be set apart, she felt sure he had been misinformed about

Heber J. Grant

her abilities, so she told him she'd be happy to do her best in whatever he asked her to do, but she wanted him to know that she had a limited education, and very little money and social position, and she was afraid she wouldn't be the example that the women of the Relief Society would expect in a leader. She finished by saying 'I'm just a humble woman!' President Grant answered, 'Sister Louizy, 85% of the women of our Church are humble women. We are calling you to be the leader of them.' "[12]

Encouraged by President Grant's words, Sister Robison shared her unique gifts and served wholeheartedly, first as a counselor and then as president. She was wise, compassionate, and hardworking. Her lack of formal education and material wealth enabled her to understand and help those in similar circumstances. Her advice to homemakers and mothers was practical and empathetic. She understood the struggle to live on a meager budget, and yet she knew the importance of a mother's influence in the home. So she encouraged

"We . . . urge, earnestly and always upon the people, the paramount necessity of living righteously; of avoiding extravagance; of cultivating habits of thrift, economy, and industry; of living strictly within their incomes; and of laying aside something, however small the amount may be, for the times of greater stress that may come to us."

First Presidency (Heber J. Grant, Anthony W. Ivins, J. Reuben Clark Jr.)

Deseret News, *Sept. 2, 1933, Church section, 7; punctuation standardized*

Relief Society sisters in California preserving food for their stake's welfare program, about 1940

However, she joined with priesthood leaders in saying that Church members needed to continue to foster fundamental values of self-sufficiency. She said: "For ninety-three years Relief Society has been saying that we take care of our needy ones. I wonder if we are leaving it too much to the Government now."[14]

In April 1936, the First Presidency introduced a Churchwide welfare program. This put the Church in a better position to help needy members. In the October 1936 general conference, President Heber J. Grant explained the purpose of the program.

"Our primary purpose," he said, "was to set up, in so far as it might be possible, a system under which the curse of idleness would be done away with, the evils of a dole abolished, and independence, industry, thrift and self respect be once more established amongst our people. The aim of the Church is to help the people to help themselves. Work is to be re-enthroned as the ruling principle of the lives of our Church membership."[15]

Years later, President Thomas S. Monson, the sixteenth President of the Church, echoed this teaching. "Remember," he said, "Church assistance is designed to help people help themselves. The rehabilitation of members is the responsibility of the individual and the family, aided by the priesthood quorum and Relief Society. We are attempting to develop

mothers to do all they could to stay at home with their children rather than leave them for the workplace.

The United States government established many relief programs to try to turn the tide on the economic crisis. For a time, the Relief Society Social Service Department worked with these community agencies to serve needy families, but needs grew beyond the capacity of the department to handle. One worker in the department saw her caseload grow from 78 families in 1929 to more than 700 in 1934.[13]

The Church appreciated the efforts of government agencies. Sister Robison said that the United States government was "doing a wonderful thing" in helping people in need.

independence, not dependence. The bishop seeks to build integrity, self-respect, dignity, and soundness of character in each person assisted, leading to complete self-sufficiency."[16]

One of the guiding principles of the welfare program was that Relief Society sisters and priesthood brethren should work in harmony. President Harold B. Lee, the eleventh President of the Church, helped establish the welfare program when he was serving as a stake president. He said:

"The most important object that is to be achieved by [the Church welfare program] is the promoting of a spirit of cooperation and unity throughout the entire Church. . . .

"To the extent that Relief Society Organizations in Wards are operating in cooperation with Priesthood Quorums and Bishoprics, just to that extent is there a [welfare] program in that ward."[17]

The role of the ward Relief Society president was especially important, said Bishop Joseph L. Wirthlin, then the Presiding Bishop of the Church: "To my way of thinking, there is only one individual who can go into a home, analyze its needs, and supply them wisely. That individual is one we may choose to call a home manager, a Relief Society president. . . . After all, these splendid women have homes of their own, have gone through the experiences related to motherhood and the management of homes."[18]

Relief Societies were well positioned to take a prominent role in ward welfare efforts. Under the direction of bishops, they appraised the needs of families and then provided dried and preserved fruits and vegetables, clothing, and bedding as needed. For a time, sisters who bottled fruit were asked to give up every tenth jar to the welfare program. Sister Belle S. Spafford, the ninth Relief Society general president, remembered gathering fruit that the wind had blown to the ground, preserving it in bottles, and giving it to sisters in need. Through this opportunity for service, she gained a greater appreciation for the purpose of Relief Society.

Relief Society leaders were an integral part of the Church welfare system. On the general, stake, and ward levels, they participated in

A gathering of Relief Society sisters in Del Rio, Texas, about 1950

welfare committee meetings, and they influenced decisions and coordinated efforts. This coordination was essential as the Church's welfare system of farms, factories, distribution centers, and other physical facilities grew. The Relief Society Social Service Department was incorporated into Church Welfare and Social Services in 1969.

Strengthening the Bonds of Charity

From 1939 to 1945, World War II engulfed much of the world. Most of the Church's programs were affected by this global conflict.

In March 1940, President J. Reuben Clark Jr., First Counselor to President Heber J. Grant, met with auxiliary presidents to reexamine all programs and activities. They outlined four basic aims for each arm of the Church: "to curtail the 'evermounting burden' on members of sustaining church activities, to lessen the bishops' burdens, to cut programs that required large, expensive meetinghouses, and to keep the Church within its income." The Relief Society and other organizations were asked to "consolidate, cooperate, eliminate, simplify, and adjust their work so as to cooperate with the [First] Presidency in reaching the aims above indicated."[19]

CLARISSA S. WILLIAMS
Sixth Relief Society General President

"Through our organization the gospel has been preached, the needy have been looked after, the sick have been comforted, the downhearted have been cheered, a message of love and of blessing has ever emanated from Relief Society workers. . . . The greatest thing in the world is love. And if we keep that always in our hearts, and give it as a message to those about us, we will be blessed and will be instruments in blessing those with whom we associate."

Clarissa S. Williams

Relief Society Magazine, *June 1922, 312*

Safeguarding the Family

Church leaders' primary purpose for simplifying their programs was to safeguard the family. Priesthood and auxiliary leaders were concerned that World War II was fragmenting homes and families. As men went to war, women had to sustain their families without immediate help from their husbands and older sons. Church leaders again encouraged mothers with children at home to find ways, if possible, to provide for the children without working outside the home full-time. These leaders encouraged Relief Society sisters to develop foundational skills of self-reliance: quilting, sewing clothing, growing gardens, and preserving and storing fruits and vegetables. They also emphasized the mother's spiritual role in the home. Nations torn by war needed good young citizens who learned lessons of morality and uprightness from their mothers.

Collaborating with Community Organizations and Priesthood Brethren

As in the previous world war, Relief Society members in the United States answered a call to volunteer and to support the efforts of other worthy organizations. In 1942, more than 10,000 Relief Society sisters completed Red Cross courses in home nursing, first aid, and nutrition. Also, the Church advocated anti-tobacco and anti-liquor campaigns to protect the health of Latter-day Saints serving in the military. Through their support of these programs and through their compassionate, charitable service, Relief Society sisters promoted good health and goodwill.

This was a time of much collaboration for Relief Society sisters, both in the community and with priesthood leaders. Sister Amy Brown Lyman, who served as the eighth Relief Society general president during most of World War II, said:

"I think that one of the things that I have appreciated as much as anything . . . is the support that the Relief Society women have always received from the priesthood—from the General Authorities of the Church and also from the local priesthood as well, especially from the ward bishops.

"The General Authorities have given the Mormon women leaders of the auxiliary organizations not only exceptional opportunities within the Church, but they have encouraged them in their cooperative work with other humanitarian agencies."[20]

One example of this cooperation was the Indian student placement program, which began in 1947 with the support of Elder Spencer W. Kimball, then of the Quorum of the Twelve Apostles. Through this program, American Indian youth from small communities accepted invitations to live for a time with Latter-day Saint families in places where formal education was readily available and where the Church was well established. The program encouraged these youth to expand their experiences, and it also promoted understanding between different cultures.

Relief Society leaders, especially Sister Belle S. Spafford, the ninth Relief Society general president, helped administer the program under the direction of Elder Kimball. Many sisters served the youth directly by nurturing them as if they were their own children. The program continued until 1996. President Boyd K. Packer of the Quorum of the Twelve Apostles later observed: "The Indian Placement program filled its purpose, and it has been disbanded. And that happens. . . . We take the scaffolding down when construction is complete."[21]

"The Pure Love of Christ": Charity in Action

Relief Society sisters in Europe experienced great devastation from World War II. They also demonstrated praiseworthy courage in serving one another in spite of harrowing conditions. They continued faithful and relied on their testimonies and the Atonement of Jesus Christ. Their lives and testimonies from this period are truly inspiring.

After the war, Maria Speidel, who served as the president of the Germany Stuttgart District Relief Society, wrote:

"The past five years have been difficult ones and we have become very humble. Our trust in the Lord and our testimony of his Church have been our pillar of strength. He has kept us mercifully, and although there was much to suffer, he has given to us a measure of his strength. Some of us have lost all our earthly possessions, every tangible thing ever dear to us, and when we say 'It is better to walk with God in the darkness than without him in the light,' we know whereof we speak. . . .

". . . With joy we sing the songs of Zion and put our trust in the Lord. He maketh all things well."[22]

Gertrude Zippro, another district Relief Society president, walked with God in the darkness many nights to love and serve her sisters. She lived in Holland at a time when the country was under military occupation. Because guards often stopped and searched travelers, she carried identification with her so she could visit branch Relief Societies in the district.

Sister Zippro's son John said that it "became increasingly dangerous to be out at night as the occupation continued for five years." Remembering his mother's dedication, he said, "Can you imagine my mother braving those

Gertrude Zippro, center, with her sisters and children

circumstances and going out at night on her bike many times, to visit another branch?" He recalled: "No matter how she felt or what the circumstances, she would take care of her obligation. What a great woman and leader she was! There is no doubt in my mind now that she was hand-picked by the Lord to be the Relief Society President at that time."

Sister Zippro's son observed, "She must have had complete trust in the Lord to go time after time under those conditions, not knowing what problems she would encounter."[23]

In Denmark, the Saints' situation was more tolerable than in many other countries. Food was available to them, so they shared it with their less-fortunate neighbors. Eva M. Gregersen, president of the Danish Mission Relief Society, said: "We have during the war taken up the work of helping our starving brother-land, Norway. Together with the mission office, we have been giving money to this purpose and every month many nice packages with food have been sent to our brothers and sisters in Norway, who have been thankful beyond words." [24]

President Hugh B. Brown was a firsthand witness of such charity. He served as president of the British Mission from 1937 to 1939, as coordinator for Latter-day Saint servicemen in Europe from 1939 to 1945, and again as president of the British Mission from 1945 to 1946. He later served as a member of the Quorum of the Twelve Apostles and the First Presidency. He reported on the service he saw among Relief Society sisters during World War II:

"There are hundreds of Relief Society women in the war zone who have been exposed to dangers, trials and hardships, comparable to that which our men undergo in the battle field. These brave women have carried on in the face of almost insuperable difficulties. . . .

"To kneel in prayer with these women and to hear them thank God for their simple blessings, for the preservation of their lives and the lives of their loved ones, and for their scanty provisions and their windowless homes is at once an inspiration and a reproof to many of us whose material blessings far exceed any enjoyed here, but who frequently complain at being deprived of a few luxuries." [25]

Hedwig Biereichel, a sister in East Germany, provided food for starving Russian prisoners of war, even though she and her family could have been imprisoned or shot for such an act

AMY BROWN LYMAN
Eighth Relief Society General President

"Little did the original members of the organization realize . . . how great their beloved Society would become."

Amy Brown Lyman

Relief Society Magazine, *Mar. 1944, 139*

"Charity is the pure love of Christ, and it endureth forever" (Moroni 7:47).

of charity.[26] Years later, she was interviewed about her experiences, as were several others who had endured similar trials during World War II. At the end of each interview, the interviewer asked, "How did you keep a testimony during all these trials?" The interviewer summarized all the responses she received with this statement: "I didn't keep a testimony through those times—the testimony kept me."[27]

When World War II ended in 1945, Relief Society sisters worldwide had suffered much sorrow and deprivation. Through it all, however, they had continued to serve one another, strengthen families, and bolster testimonies.

As a witness of so much suffering and so much selfless service, Sister Amy Brown Lyman declared:

"[My] testimony has been my anchor and my stay, my satisfaction in times of joy and gladness, my comfort in times of sorrow and discouragement. . . .

"I am grateful for the opportunity I have had of serving . . . in the Relief Society where during most of my mature life I have worked so happily and contentedly with its thousands of members. I have visited in their homes, slept in their beds, and eaten at their tables, and have thus learned of their beauty of character, their unselfishness, their understanding hearts, their faithfulness, and their sacrifices. I honor beyond my power of expression this great sisterhood of service."[28]

In times of trial and uncertainty, Relief Society sisters worldwide have followed Mormon's admonition to "cleave unto charity, which is the greatest of all." They have demonstrated their sure understanding that while "all things must fail . . . charity is the pure love of Christ, and it endureth forever."[29] Time and time again, they have been true to their motto: "Charity never faileth."

A Worldwide Circle of Sisterhood

This great circle of sisters will be a protection for each of you and for your families. The Relief Society might be likened to a refuge—the place of safety and protection—the sanctuary of ancient times. You will be safe within it. It encircles each sister like a protecting wall.

Boyd K. Packer

A Worldwide Circle of Sisterhood

When the Prophet Joseph Smith met with Relief Society sisters in Nauvoo, he taught that in addition to giving temporal service, they were to strengthen people spiritually (see chapter 2). With this counsel as a foundation, Relief Society sisters have found love and safety from the storms of life as they have served together. They have shared the gospel of Jesus Christ with each other and with those around them. Relief Society has become a shelter from the world—a place of refuge—and a center of light to the world—a place of influence.

In a Relief Society meeting in Ogden, Utah, Sister Eliza R. Snow, the second Relief Society general president, gratefully acknowledged sisters' efforts to strengthen one another temporally and spiritually. She told them that although the Church did not keep a record of every donation they made to help those in need, the Lord kept a perfect record of their saving work:

"I am well aware that a great deal is donated that never reaches the [record] books. President Joseph Smith said this society was organized to save souls. What have the sisters done to win

Relief Society sisters find love and safety from the storms of life as they serve together.

back those who have gone astray?—to warm up the hearts of those who have grown cold in the gospel?—Another book is kept of your faith, your kindness, your good works, and words. Another record is kept. Nothing is lost."[1]

A heavenly record is kept of the work of Relief Society sisters as they reach out to those whose hearts have grown cold and who need faith, kindness, good works, and good words.

Worldwide Sisterhood

In the mid-1900s, as the world suffered the effects of wars and natural disasters, the Relief Society's work continued to expand. True to the purposes of the organization—increasing faith and personal righteousness, strengthening families and homes, and seeking out and helping those in need—the Relief Society provided a refuge for Latter-day Saint sisters and was an influence for good. In 1947 the general Relief Society presidency (Sisters Belle S. Spafford, Marianne Sharp, and Gertrude Garff) taught, "Ours is a healing mission requiring the larger heart, the kindlier touch, the steadier will."[2]

At that time, some governments established political restrictions and even built some physical barriers. These restrictions and barriers, known by names such as the Iron Curtain and the Berlin Wall, were designed to restrict some people and exclude others. In contrast, Relief Society sisters built spiritual walls of refuge designed to protect and include. They came together in a worldwide circle of sisterhood and invited others to join them.

Even in countries with political boundaries and laws that prevented open participation in religion, members of Relief Societies felt a connection to their sisters throughout the world. They quietly remained true to their testimonies of the restored gospel and to the purposes of Relief Society.

In 1980, President Boyd K. Packer of the Quorum of the Twelve Apostles and his wife, Donna, visited a Relief Society in Czechoslovakia (now the Czech Republic and Slovakia). He later recalled:

"It was not easy to obtain visas, and we used great care so as not to jeopardize the safety and well-being of our members, who for generations had struggled to keep their faith alive under conditions of unspeakable oppression.

"The most memorable meeting was held in an upper room. The blinds were drawn. Even at night, those attending came at different times, one from one direction and one from another, so as to not call attention to themselves.

"There were in attendance 12 sisters. We sang the hymns of Zion from songbooks—words without music—printed more than 50 years before. [A lesson] was reverently given from the pages of a handmade manual. . . .

"I told those sisters that they belonged to the largest and by all measure the greatest women's organization on earth. I quoted the Prophet Joseph Smith when he and the Brethren organized the Relief Society. . . .

"The Spirit was there. The lovely sister who had conducted with gentility and reverence wept openly.

"I told them that upon our return I was assigned to speak at a Relief Society conference; could I deliver a message from them? Several

Members of the Relief Society come together in a circle of sisterhood.

of them made notes; each expression, every one, was in the spirit of giving—not of asking for anything. I shall never forget what one sister wrote: 'A small circle of sisters send their own hearts and thoughts to all the sisters and begs the Lord to help us go forward.'

"Those words, *circle of sisters,* inspired me. I could see them standing in a circle that reached beyond that room and circled the world."[3]

Recalling that meeting, President Packer said, "I stood, for a moment, in that circle and felt the impulses of faith and courage and love coming and going on either side."[4]

Such faith and courage and love combine to form the heritage of Relief Society sisters everywhere. President Henry B. Eyring, a counselor in the First Presidency, encouraged Relief Society sisters to share this heritage. "You pass the heritage along as you help others receive the gift of charity in their hearts," he said. "They will then be able to pass it to others. The history of Relief Society is recorded in words and numbers, but the heritage is passed heart to heart."[5] This happens in Relief Society's circle of sisterhood.

A Place of Refuge

Since the early days of Relief Society, sisters have provided a place of refuge—a place of healing, love, kindness, care, and belonging. In Nauvoo, sisters found refuge in Relief Society as they relied on each others' faith and skills and as they shared food and clothing. This continued as they crossed the plains and as they established themselves in the Utah Territory. Now, as the Church grows throughout the world, sisters continue to find refuge in Relief Society.

President Boyd K. Packer said: "This great circle of sisters will be a protection for each of you and for your families. The Relief Society might be likened to a refuge—the place of safety and protection—the sanctuary of ancient times. You will be safe within it. It encircles each sister like a protecting wall."[6]

In 1999, Bobbie Sandberg, a young wife and mother, moved with her family from the United States to Taiwan. Although she would be there for only six months while she and her

BELLE S. SPAFFORD
Ninth Relief Society General President

"Through the years, Relief Society has been just as constant in its purpose as truth is constant. The purposes that were important for a handful of women in Nauvoo are still important to women world-wide. That is the miracle of Relief Society. I've worked in Relief Society many years, and I'm just beginning to get an insight into its greatness."

Belle S Spafford

Ensign, *June 1974, 15*

"No matter where [a family may] go, a Church family awaits them" (Boyd K. Packer).

transportation she could find. She rode her bicycle through the rubble until she had visited many sisters in the ward.

In the midst of physical turmoil, Sister Sandberg was under the safe protection of a Relief Society. Her Relief Society president cared about the safety and needs of each sister in her ward.

Like Sister Sandberg, many Latter-day Saints around the world can attest to the truth of this statement by President Packer: "How consoling it is to know that no matter where [a family may] go, a Church family awaits them. From the day they arrive, he will belong to a quorum of the priesthood and she will belong to Relief Society."[7]

husband taught an English class, her Taiwanese sisters encircled her in the protective influence of Relief Society.

This protection was especially evident when a terrible earthquake shook the country, with its epicenter near the Sandbergs' home. Buildings tumbled down on both sides of the school where they lived. Within hours of the first big jolt, Sister Sandberg's Relief Society president came to the family like an angel of mercy to assess their needs and help them. Because many of the roads and buildings had been destroyed and all communication lines were down, this caring president used the only means of

A Place of Influence

Sister Belle S. Spafford was called as the ninth Relief Society general president in April 1945, and President George Albert Smith was set apart as the eighth President of the Church about six weeks later. President Smith encouraged Sister Spafford and all Relief Society sisters to provide temporal support for people who continued to suffer from the effects of World War II. He also asked them to make their influence felt among all the women of the world. He said, "When the Prophet Joseph Smith turned the key for the emancipation of womankind, it was turned for all the world."[8]

The Relief Society Building, a Center of Influence

In October 1945, plans were announced to erect a Relief Society building.[9] In October 1947, the First Presidency approved a plan proposed by Sister Belle S. Spafford: each member of the Relief Society, which then numbered 100,000, was asked to donate five dollars to the project. Sisters from all over the world sent donations. Some sent artifacts from their homelands to beautify the interior of the building. In one year, sisters raised $554,016.

Sister Spafford declared: "This achievement represents great monetary value, but not monetary value alone. Herein are represented many intangible values—values of supreme worth—appreciation for the honored position accorded women in the gospel plan; testimony of the divinity of the work of the society; and gratitude for the opportunity given the sisters of the Church to serve . . . ; loyalty to leadership; unselfish devotion to a great cause. It is a reflection of the greatness that is inherent within the society."[10]

The building, located just northeast of the Salt Lake Temple, was dedicated on October 3, 1956. In the dedicatory prayer, President David O. McKay, the ninth President of the Church, spoke of the worldwide influence that would emanate from the building: "To make more effective their service to the needy and

Relief Society Building, Salt Lake City, Utah, 1956

suffering to those in the Church and in the World, the Relief Society has erected with the aid of the Church membership this beautiful Relief Society home."[11]

Since 1984 the building has also housed the offices of the Young Women general presidency and the Primary general presidency.

Influence among Those of Other Faiths

Sister Spafford learned a great lesson from President George Albert Smith about sharing the Church's values with the women of the world. Soon after she was sustained as Relief Society general president, "a letter came from the National Council of Women, announcing their annual meeting to be held in New York City.

"Sister Spafford had attended those meetings before, and in view of her previous experience, she and her counselors carefully considered the invitation for several weeks.

"They decided to recommend to the President of the Church that the Relief Society terminate its membership in those councils. They prepared a statement of recommendation, listing all of the reasons for so doing.

"Trembling and uncertain, Sister Spafford placed the paper on the desk of President George Albert Smith, saying, 'The Relief Society Presidency wishes to recommend that the General Board terminate its membership in the National Council and in the International Council of Women, for the reasons listed on this paper.'

"President Smith carefully read the paper. Had they not held membership for well over half a century? he inquired.

"Sister Spafford explained how costly it was to go to New York, the time it took, and described the humiliation they occasionally experienced. She recommended that they withdraw because 'we don't get a thing from these councils.'

"This wise, old prophet tipped back in his chair and looked at her with a disturbed expression. 'You want to withdraw because you don't get anything out of it?' he questioned.

"'That is our feeling,' she replied.

"'Tell me,' he said, 'what is it that you are putting into it?

"'Sister Spafford,' he continued, 'you surprise me. Do you always think in terms of what you get? Don't you think also in terms of what you have to give?'

"He returned that paper to her and extended his hand. With considerable firmness he said, 'You continue your membership in these councils and make your influence felt.'"[12]

She did make her influence felt. She participated in the National Council of Women and the International Council of Women and held

Sister Belle S. Spafford, left, at an International Council of Women convention

leadership positions in those organizations for years. She stood strong for the principles of the gospel of Jesus Christ and for the purposes of Relief Society.

Every time Sister Spafford went to the International Council of Women (ICW), she was assigned to the "social and moral welfare" session. She recounted:

"At one time I protested going back into the social and moral welfare [session], and I was very friendly at that time with the ICW president. . . . I said, 'I go all the time to this session, and it's just getting so sordid that I'd like a change.' She said, 'Well, you're certainly entitled to one, and I'll see that you get it.'

"Then she came back and said, 'We can't grant your request because your own council insists that you remain in the social and moral welfare.' She said, 'It may be of interest to you to know the reason. Your national president says you always stand by the position of your Church in these matters and they know the position of the Mormon Church and they feel there is safety in having you there.' " [13]

Women in these organizations knew that their friend Belle Spafford would stand by the Church's principles, and they needed that kind of wisdom and strength. In 1954 she was chosen as the leader of the United States delegation at the International Council of Women in Helsinki, Finland. As she led a grand march

at the opening of the conference, her thoughts went back in time:

"As I looked out at the glittering audience made up of people of many nations . . . , my mind suddenly flashed back to the words of our pioneer [Relief Society] leaders . . . 'standing as we do at the head of the women of the world,' . . . 'for the rights of the women of Zion and the rights of the women of all nations.' . . . I knew that our pioneer women leaders had been given by divine insight a knowledge of the destiny of Relief Society. . . . It is my conviction that

Relief Society sisters and full-time missionaries in San Antonio, Texas, about 1950

the time had come for Relief Society's influence to be felt worldwide among womankind."[14]

In 1987 the First Presidency counseled the Relief Society to withdraw from the National Council of Women and the International Council of Women. The time had come for the Relief Society general presidency to focus more energy on their rapidly growing worldwide organization rather than on other nationwide and worldwide causes. But as the Church has grown, Latter-day Saint women have continued to make their influence felt all over the world—in their communities, schools, and worthy local organizations. They have followed the pattern established by President Smith and Sister Spafford, thinking in terms of what they can give, not what they might get.

Nurturing and Teaching Investigators and New Converts

With the worldwide growth of the Church, Relief Society has been a place of influence for investigators and new converts. This influence has included giving new members opportunities to serve and lead. Sister Silvia H. Allred, a counselor in the Relief Society general presidency, told of her mother, Hilda Alvarenga, serving as a branch Relief Society president in San Salvador, El Salvador:

"My mother was a recent convert to the Church when she was called to be the Relief Society president in our small branch in San Salvador. She told the branch president that she was inexperienced, unprepared, and inadequate. She was in her 30s, had very

"When we qualify ourselves by our worthiness, when we strive with faith nothing wavering to fulfill the duties appointed to us, when we seek the inspiration of the Almighty in the performance of our responsibilities, we can achieve the miraculous."

Thomas S. Monson

In Conference Report, Apr. 1988, 52; or Ensign, May 1988, 43

little formal education, and her whole life had been devoted to the care of her husband and seven children. But the branch president called her anyway.

"I watched my mother rise to the occasion. While serving, she learned leadership skills and developed new gifts such as teaching, public speaking, and planning and organizing meetings, activities, and service projects. She influ-enced the women in the branch. She served them and taught them to serve one another. The sisters loved and respected her. She helped other women to discover, use, and develop gifts and talents; she helped them become builders of the kingdom and of strong, spiritual families. She stayed faithful to the temple covenants she made. When she passed away, she was at peace with her Maker.

Hilda Alvarenga

"A sister who served with her as a counselor in the Relief Society wrote me a letter years later: 'Your mother was the person who taught me the way to become what I am now. From her, I learned charity, kindness, honesty, and responsibility in our callings. She was my mentor and my example. I am now 80 years old, but I have stayed faithful to the Savior and His gospel. I have served a mission, and the Lord has blessed me greatly.'"[15]

This devoted Relief Society president helped strengthen the testimonies of sisters who were already members of the branch. She also nur-tured the faith of women who were investigating the Church and those who had recently been baptized and confirmed. She led efforts to make Relief Society a welcoming, nurturing place.

Influencing Others by Sharing the Gospel

Not long after President and Sister Packer visited that small circle of sisters in Czecho-slovakia, a young woman who was searching for spiritual refuge, love, and meaning in her life was drawn into that very circle. Her name was Olga Kovářová, and at the time she was a doctoral student at a university in the city of Brno. The university imposed the teachings of atheism on students. Olga felt that students and others all around her were directionless. She hungered for a deeper spiritual life, and she sensed that same hunger among her friends and colleagues.

During Olga's time at the university, she met Otakar Vojkůvka, a 75-year-old Latter-day Saint man. She later recalled: "He appeared to me seventy-five in his age but in his heart nearer eighteen and full of joy. This was so unusual in Czechoslovakia at that time of cynicism. . . . I saw that he was not only educated but knew how to live joyfully." She asked him and his family about the meaning of life, and

Like the Savior's ancient Apostles, Relief Society sisters can be instruments in God's hands.

eventually they introduced her to other Church members. She wanted to know how they found joy and where they read about God. They gave her a copy of the Book of Mormon, which she began reading eagerly.

Olga was converted to the restored gospel, and she decided to be baptized. She had to be baptized in the woods at night to avoid drawing attention to a religious activity. Unfortunately, many fishermen were in the woods on the night of her baptism. But after Olga and her friends waited and finally offered an earnest prayer, the fishermen left.

A Church member who attended Olga's baptism asked her, "Do you know why there were many fishermen by the water tonight?" Then he said, "Remember that Jesus, as he walked by the Sea of Galilee, said to Simon Peter and Andrew, who were casting a net into the sea, 'Follow me, and I will make you fishers of men.'" Olga felt that "his meaning was that I should soon be an instrument in God's hands to bring young people into the Church."

Olga did exactly that. She influenced many who were searching for truth and happiness. Because proselyting was not allowed in their country, she and the Vojkůvka family conducted a class they called "School of Wisdom." In these settings, they taught moral and ethical values to help people find spirituality and joy in life. Many of their students felt the influence of the Spirit, and opportunities often opened for discussions with selected individuals about Heavenly Father and the gospel of Jesus Christ.[16]

Later, when Sister Barbara W. Winder was serving as the eleventh Relief Society general president, she had the opportunity to travel to Czechoslovakia with her husband, Richard W. Winder, who had served there as a young missionary years earlier. As they entered a home where a meeting would be held, a vibrant young woman approached them enthusiastically and said, "Welcome! My name is Olga, and I am the Relief Society president." Brother and Sister Winder noted the light in her countenance and the Spirit of the Lord upon her. As the Relief Society president of her little branch, Olga Kovářová was an influence for good in a world of political oppression and religious persecution, and she helped provide refuge

ELAINE L. JACK
Twelfth Relief Society General President

"We are part of a grand whole. We need each other to make our sisterhood complete. When we reach out to clasp the hands of our sisters, we reach to every continent, for we are of every nation. We are bonded as we try to understand what the Lord has to say to us, what He will make of us. We speak in different tongues, yet we are a family who can still be of one heart."

Ensign, *May 1992, 91*

for those who joined the Church and became members of Relief Society. She helped save the souls of others by bringing them to Christ.

Sister Kovářová's conversion story and her missionary work are a partial fulfillment of a prophecy of President Spencer W. Kimball, the twelfth President of the Church: "Much of the major growth that is coming to the Church in the last days will come because many of the good women of the world (in whom there is often such an inner sense of spirituality) will be drawn to the Church in large numbers. This will happen to the degree that the women of the Church reflect righteousness and articulateness in their lives and to the degree that the women of the Church are seen as distinct and different—in happy ways—from the women of the world."[17]

Influencing Others through Service

In 1992, sisters all over the world celebrated the 150th anniversary of the Relief Society by participating in service projects in their communities. Through this effort, organized under the direction of general and local priesthood leaders, sisters shared the influence of Relief Society worldwide. Sister Elaine L. Jack, who was serving as the twelfth Relief Society general president at the time, said:

"We asked each of our local units to look to the needs of their own community and to decide what community service would be needed the most. Can you imagine what that did in this world?

"One of our Relief Society presidents went to the city council in a California city and said, 'What are the things that you feel are needed in this community that we could do?' And the men said, 'You mean 20,000 groups throughout this world are going to be doing this same thing?' And she said yes. And [one of the council members] said, 'You'll change the world.' And I think we did . . . for the better. That was one of the unifying things. And [there was] such a variety of service. . . . [Sisters]

Service can change the world for the better.

made lap rugs in South Africa for those elderly in the home. . . . They planted flowers around [a] clock tower in Samoa. And they did so many things with homeless shelters or providing books for children or painting homes for unwed mothers, that sort of thing. We felt that throughout the world these community service projects were a great thing, both for the sisters and for the community."[18]

Influencing Others through Literacy

As Relief Society sisters organized community service projects, Sister Jack and her counselors focused on a worldwide service effort: helping sisters learn to read. "We felt that women throughout the world needed to be able to read, and there were many who could not," she said. "Can you imagine—if they didn't know how to read, how could they teach their children, how could they improve their circumstances, how could they study the gospel? So we thought that there would be nothing that could be more beneficial than to promote a literacy effort. . . . But also our purpose was to encourage lifelong learning for every sister."[19]

President Thomas S. Monson, the sixteenth President of the Church, once met a woman in Monroe, Louisiana, who had been blessed by this Relief Society service and who had shared the blessing with others. She approached him in an airport and said: "President Monson,

Thomas S. Monson

before I joined the Church and became a member of the Relief Society, I could not read. I could not write. None of my family could." She told President Monson that Relief Society sisters had taught her to read and that now she helped others learn to read. After talking with her, President Monson "reflected on the supreme happiness she must have felt when she opened her Bible and read for the first time the words of the Lord. . . . That day in Monroe, Louisiana," he said, "I received a confirmation by the Spirit of your exalted objective of improving literacy among your sisters."[20]

Influencing and Strengthening Sisters in Wards and Branches

Even as faithful Relief Society sisters have made their influence felt in their communities and throughout the world, they have not forgotten to strengthen each other in their own wards and branches. Sister Julie B. Beck, who later served as the fifteenth Relief Society general president, found sisterhood, refuge, and influence in Relief Society when she was a young, inexperienced mother and homemaker. She recalled:

"Relief Society should be organized, aligned, and mobilized to strengthen families and help

The ability to read helps women improve their circumstances, study the gospel, and teach their children.

"You are members of the greatest women's organi-zation in the world, an organization which is a vital part of the kingdom of God on earth and which is so designed and operated that it helps its faithful members to gain eternal life in our Father's kingdom."

Joseph Fielding Smith
Relief Society Magazine, *Dec. 1970, 883*

our homes to be sacred sanctuaries from the world. I learned this years ago when I was newly married. My parents, who had been my neighbors, announced that they would be moving to another part of the world. I had relied on my mother's nurturing, wise, and en-couraging example. Now she was going to be gone for a long time. This was before e-mail, fax machines, cell phones, and Web cameras, and mail delivery was notoriously slow. One day before she left, I sat weeping with her and asked, 'Who will be my mother?' Mother thought carefully, and with the Spirit and power of revelation which comes to women of this kind, she said

A Relief Society choir singing in the Salt Lake Tabernacle, 1956

to me, 'If I never come back, if you never see me again, if I'm never able to teach you another thing, you tie yourself to Relief Society. Relief Society will be your mother.'

"Mother knew that if I was sick, the sisters would take care of me, and when I had my babies, they would help me. But my mother's greatest hope was that the sisters in Relief Society would be powerful, spiritual leaders for me. I began from that time to learn abundantly from women of stature and faith."[21]

An Ever-Expanding Circle of Sisters

The first time President Boyd K. Packer publicly told of his experience with the Relief Society sisters in Czechoslovakia, he was

Boyd K. Packer

speaking at the general Relief Society meeting in 1980. He said, "I caught then the vision of a great circle of sisters."[22] In 1998 he shared the experience again, this time in a general conference address to the entire Church. He observed, "The Relief Society is more than a circle now; it is more like a fabric of lace spread across the continents."[23]

Relief Society sisters are part of a divinely inspired organization that the Prophet Joseph Smith established under priesthood authority. As women participate in Relief Society and devote themselves to it, they will continue to provide refuge and sisterhood and be powerful influences for good. President Packer promised great blessings to sisters who serve in this cause:

"Your every need shall be fulfilled, now, and in the eternities; every neglect will be erased; every abuse will be corrected. All of this can come to you, and come quickly, when you devote yourself to Relief Society.

"Service in the Relief Society magnifies and sanctifies each individual sister. Your membership in Relief Society should be ever with you. When you devote yourself to the Relief Society and organize it and operate it and participate in it, you sustain the cause that will bless every woman who comes within its influence."[24]

Strengthening Sisterhood through Expressions of Charity

In an address to Relief Society sisters, President Thomas S. Monson shared thoughts about how expressions of charity strengthen the ties of sisterhood in Relief Society:

"I consider charity—or 'the pure love of Christ'—to be the opposite of criticism and judging. In speaking of charity, I do not at this moment have in mind the relief of the suffering through the giving of our substance. That, of course, is necessary and proper. Tonight, however, I have in mind the charity that manifests itself when we are tolerant of others and lenient toward their actions, the kind of charity that forgives, the kind of charity that is patient.

"I have in mind the charity that impels us to be sympathetic, compassionate, and merciful, not only in times of sickness and affliction and distress but also in times of weakness or error on the part of others."

"True charity is love in action. The need for charity is everywhere" (Thomas S. Monson).

"There is a serious need for the charity that gives attention to those who are unnoticed, hope to those who are discouraged, aid to those who are afflicted. True charity is love in action. The need for charity is everywhere.

"Needed is the charity which refuses to find satisfaction in hearing or in repeating the reports of misfortunes that come to others, unless by so doing, the unfortunate one may be benefited. . . .

"Charity is having patience with someone who has let us down. It is resisting the impulse to become offended easily. It is accepting weaknesses and shortcomings. It is accepting people as they truly are. It is looking beyond physical appearances to attributes that will not dim through time. It is resisting the impulse to categorize others.

"Charity, that pure love of Christ, is manifest when a group of young women from a singles ward travels hundreds of miles to attend the funeral services for the mother of one of their Relief Society sisters. Charity is shown when devoted visiting teachers return month after

Charity is felt in the invitation "Come—sit by us."

month, year after year to the same uninter-
ested, somewhat critical sister. It is evident
when an elderly widow is remembered and
taken to ward functions and to Relief Society
activities. It is felt when the sister sitting
alone in Relief Society receives the invitation,
'Come—sit by us.'

"In a hundred small ways, all of you wear the
mantle of charity. Life is perfect for none of us.
Rather than being judgmental and critical of
each other, may we have the pure love of Christ
for our fellow travelers in this journey through
life. May we recognize that each one is doing
her best to deal with the challenges which
come her way, and may we strive to do *our*
best to help out.

"Charity has been defined as 'the highest,
noblest, strongest kind of love,' the 'pure love
of Christ . . . ; and whoso is found possessed
of it at the last day, it shall be well with [her].'

"'Charity never faileth.' May this long-
enduring Relief Society motto, this timeless
truth, guide you in everything you do. May it
permeate your very souls and find expression
in all your thoughts and actions."[25]

"Pure Religion"

Watchcare and Ministering through Visiting Teaching

We are surrounded by those in need

of our attention, our encouragement, our

support, our comfort, our kindness. . . . We

are the Lord's hands here upon the earth,

with the mandate to serve and to lift His

children. He is dependent upon each of us.

Thomas S. Monson

Relief Society Teachers' Monthly Report

THE LORD IS ON MY SIDE

"Pure Religion"
Watchcare and Ministering through Visiting Teaching

When Jesus Christ was on the earth, He showed us the way we should live. "He marked the path and led the way," Sister Eliza R. Snow wrote.[1] He showed us how to minister—how to watch over and strengthen one another. His was a ministry to individuals, one by one. He taught that we should leave the ninety and nine to save the straying one.[2] He healed and taught individuals, even spending time with each person in a multitude of 2,500 people, allowing each to receive a personal witness of His divinity.[3]

The Savior calls His disciples to work with Him in His ministry, giving them the opportunity to serve others and become more like Him. In Relief Society, each sister has the opportunity to watch over and strengthen sisters one by one through visiting teaching. Sister Julie B. Beck, the fifteenth Relief Society general president, said, "Because we follow the example and teachings of Jesus Christ, we value this sacred assignment to love, know, serve, understand, teach, and minister in His behalf."[4]

Beginnings of Visiting Teaching: Collecting Donations and Organizing Service

In 1843, as the population of Nauvoo, Illinois, expanded, the Latter-day Saints in the city were divided into four wards. In a meeting held on July 28 of that year, Relief Society leaders appointed a visiting committee of four sisters for each ward. The visiting committees' most visible responsibilities were to assess needs and collect donations.

Through His example, the Savior taught us how to watch over and strengthen one another.

Donations included money, food, and clothing. Each week, visiting committees gave the donations they had collected to the treasurer of the Relief Society. The Relief Society used these donations to provide aid and relief for the needy.

In fulfilling this responsibility, one sister expressed her belief that "our salvation depend[s] on our liberality to the poor." Another sister expressed her agreement, saying: "The Lord confirms it again and again. He is delighted with our acts of charity."[5]

This practice continued well into the twentieth century. Generally the sisters who were assigned to go visiting went with baskets in hand, receiving items such as matches, rice, baking soda, and bottles of fruit. Most donations were used to help with local needs, but some were used to meet needs thousands of miles away. For example, after World War II, Relief Society sisters in the United States gathered, sorted, mended, and packed more than 500,000 articles of clothing and sent them to Europe.

In addition to collecting donations, visiting committees assessed the needs in the homes they visited. They reported their observations to Relief Society leaders, who organized efforts to help.

President Joseph F. Smith, the sixth President of the Church, told of a time when he saw Relief Society sisters extend unselfish, Christlike love to a family:

"It was my privilege not long ago to visit one of our settlements in an outlying Stake of Zion where a great deal of sickness prevailed at the time, and although we had been traveling many days and we reached the settlement late in the evening, we were solicited to go round with the president to visit some of the sick. We found a poor sister prostrate upon a bed of sickness, in a very critical condition. Her poor husband sat by her bedside almost distracted at the dreadful illness of his wife who was the mother of a number of little children clustered around. The family seemed to be in a very destitute condition.

"A nice matronly woman soon came into the house, carrying with her a basket containing nourishing food and some delicacies for the use of the afflicted family. On inquiry we learned that she had been detailed by the Relief Society of the ward to watch over and administer to the sick woman through the night. She was there prepared to look after the little children, to see that they were properly washed and fed and put to bed; to tidy up the house and make everything as comfortable as possible for the afflicted woman and her family. We also learned that another good sister would be detailed to relieve her the following day; and so on, from day to day, this poor, afflicted family

Visiting committees collected donations to help with local needs.

"Let us have compassion upon each other, and let the strong tenderly nurse the weak into strength, and let those who can see guide the blind until they can see the way for themselves."

Brigham Young

Teachings of Presidents of the Church: Brigham Young (1997), 219

received the kindest care and attention from the sisters of the Relief Society until health should again come to relieve the sick one from her sufferings.

"We also learned that this Relief Society was so organized and disciplined that all the sick in the settlement were receiving similar attention and ministrations for their comfort and relief. Never before had I seen so clearly exemplified the utility and beauty of this grand organization as in the example we here witnessed, and I thought what a gracious thing it was that the Lord inspired the Prophet Joseph Smith to establish such an organization in the Church."[6]

Visiting Teaching as a Spiritual Ministry

While visiting teachers have always looked after the temporal needs of individuals and families, they have also had a higher purpose. Sister Eliza R. Snow, the second Relief Society general president, taught: "I consider the office of a teacher a high and holy office. I hope the sisters do not think that it consists merely in begging for the poor. You want to be filled with the Spirit of God, of wisdom, of humility, of love, that in case they have nothing to give they may not dread your coming."

Sister Snow hoped that sisters would "perceive a difference in their houses" after a visit.[7] She counseled visiting teachers to prepare themselves spiritually before they visited homes so they would be able to ascertain and meet spiritual needs as well as temporal ones: "A teacher . . . should surely have so much of the Spirit of the Lord, as she enters a house to know what spirit she meets in there. . . . Plead before God and the Holy Ghost to get [the Spirit] so that you will be able to meet that spirit that prevails in that house . . . and you may feel to talk words of peace and comfort, and if you find a sister feeling cold, take her to your heart as you would a child to your bosom and warm [her] up."[8]

Sarah M. Kimball, who served as a ward Relief Society president in the late 1860s, shared similar counsel with the sisters in her ward: "It is the duty of teachers to visit their

Sarah M. Kimball

[assigned sisters] once a month, to inquire after the prosperity and happiness of the members. It is their duty to speak words of wisdom, of consolation and peace."[9] Relief Society leaders emphasized that visiting teachers were "not only to gather means but to teach and expound the principles of the gospel."[10] In 1916, visiting teachers were formally asked to discuss a gospel topic each month as well as providing temporal service. In 1923, the general Relief Society presidency introduced uniform monthly messages to be given by all visiting teachers.

"The Rebirth of Visiting Teaching"—"A Beautiful Experience for Women"

In 1944, eight years after the implementation of the Church's welfare plan (see chapter 5), Sister Amy Brown Lyman, the eighth Relief Society general president, began to question visiting teachers' traditional responsibility to collect donations. After studying the issue, she and her counselors recommended to the Presiding Bishopric that "the matter of collection of funds . . . should be decided by the General

Authorities of the Church rather than by the Relief Society."

Presiding Bishop LeGrand Richards took the recommendation to the First Presidency. He later reported that the First Presidency and the Bishopric felt that it was "advisable for the Relief Society to discontinue the collections of charity funds by the visiting teachers."[11]

Sister Belle S. Spafford, who was serving as Sister Lyman's second counselor at the time, shared a personal account of this change in visiting teaching:

"The Brethren said, 'No more collection of charity funds by the Relief Society visiting teacher. You will become a service organization, not a financing organization of charity relief.'

". . . I very well recall sitting one day in a meeting with members of the Relief Society presidency and the secretary and two or three of the board members, when one of the sisters said, 'They have sounded the death knell of visiting teaching. If they can't go to collect for the poor, who's going to want to go from door to door just to visit?' . . . I spoke up and I said, 'I don't believe it's the death knell. I believe it's the rebirth of visiting teaching. And I believe that countless women who have refused to serve as visiting teachers will now be glad to go when they go as friendly visitors to observe conditions in the home where there is need without making a social welfare investigation;

Visiting teachers have always strived to meet the spiritual and temporal needs of those they visit.

when they don't have to feel like they're begging for money. They will know they go to build the spirit of the home. And it will be a beautiful experience for women who need it. . . . I don't think for one minute that this is the death knell of visiting teaching.'

"It did not prove to be. From then on the program began to flourish and women who had not served before asked to be visiting teachers."[12]

Sister Spafford later served as the ninth Relief Society general president. She saw countless examples of the good that visiting teaching can bring into the lives of all Relief Society sisters. She testified:

"Some of the very fine work is done by our visiting teachers and our Relief Society presidents, because they go under the spirit of their calling and they are emissaries of Relief Society. . . . They are mothers, and they have the human understanding of other women and their sorrows. So we must not narrow our concept of the social welfare to the hungry or the poor. The Savior told us to remember the poor in spirit, didn't he? And don't the rich get sick, the same as the poor; and don't they have a hard time to find a nurse? . . . Now that's what Relief Society is supposed to be doing. I could tell you story after story after story where visiting teachers have done skilled work in alleviating trouble in a home, simply in the office of their calling."[13]

Visiting teachers in central Africa traveling to visit their sisters

A Privilege, a Duty, and a Commitment: Sharing the Vision of Visiting Teaching Worldwide

President Henry B. Eyring, a counselor in the First Presidency, testified that visiting teaching is part of the Lord's plan to provide help for people all over the world:

"The only system which could provide succor and comfort across a church so large in a world so varied would be through individual servants near the people in need. The Lord had seen that coming from the beginning of Relief Society.

"He set a pattern in place. Two Relief Society sisters accept their assignment to visit another as a call from the Lord. That was true from the start. . . .

"The members of Relief Society have always been trusted by local priesthood shepherds. Every bishop and every branch president has a Relief Society president to depend upon. She has visiting teachers, who know the trials and the needs of every sister. She can, through them, know the hearts of individuals and families. She can meet needs and help the bishop in his call to nurture individuals and families."[14]

As President Eyring observed, visiting teaching is well suited to the worldwide growth of the Church. Through this system of watchcare, each Latter-day Saint woman has the opportunity to be an instrument in the Lord's hands.

Sister Geraldine Bangerter, bottom left, with Brazilian sisters who helped establish Relief Society in their homeland

Relief Society sisters have worked diligently to establish visiting teaching throughout the world. For example, when the Church was young in Brazil, most branches did not have Relief Societies or knowledge about how to establish them. Because local leaders were unfamiliar with Relief Society, William Grant Bangerter, the mission president at the time, called his wife, Geraldine Bangerter, to be the mission Relief Society president. She was unfamiliar with the country, she had not yet gained proficiency with the language, and she had just given birth to their seventh child. Nevertheless, she started working with counselors and a secretary. With help from sister missionaries who acted as interpreters, these sisters decided that "the first thing they needed to do was teach the women how to visit each other and learn about their needs. So they said, 'We're going to teach about visiting teaching.' . . .

"They decided to start with a little branch [in] São Paulo in the industrial part of the city, whose inhabitants were mainly poor. The presidency sent word ahead to the few sisters of that branch, saying, 'Please meet us on this night at this time in the building that we rent.' "

Sister Bangerter and one of her counselors "drove across a city of twelve million people. They showed up at the branch, where . . . there were seven humble women."

After the sisters began the meeting with a song and a prayer, one of Sister Bangerter's counselors stood to teach about visiting teaching. "She held a little paper; she trembled so much it was shaking. She got up and read her message. It lasted five minutes.

"She sat down, and they all turned to look at [Sister Bangerter], who said, 'I don't speak Portuguese.' But they wanted her to be their teacher. No one in the room spoke English. She stood up and said all the Portuguese she knew. It came out as a four-sentence paragraph:

" 'Eu sei que Deus vive.' I know that God lives.

" 'Eu sei que Jesus é o Cristo.' I know that Jesus is the Christ.

"'Eu sei que esta é a igreja verdadeira.' I know this is the true church.

"'Em nome de Jesus Cristo, amém.' In the name of Jesus Christ, amen.

"That was the first Relief Society meeting held in that branch—a five-minute talk on visiting teaching from a sister who'd never *had* a visiting teacher, *seen* a visiting teacher, or *been* a visiting teacher, [followed by] a testimony of the gospel.

"... Out of that little group and others like them has grown a wonderful, vibrant, faith-filled body of women in the country of Brazil. They're talented, educated, intelligent, fabulous leaders, and they would never be what they are without the gospel of Jesus Christ and their faith."[15]

Visiting teaching has become a vehicle for Latter-day Saint women worldwide to love, nurture, and serve—to "act according to those sympathies which God has planted in your bosoms," as Joseph Smith taught.[16]

Dedicated visiting teachers answer the call from latter-day prophets to give Christlike service. President Spencer W. Kimball, the twelfth President of the Church, taught: "God does notice us, and he watches over us. But it is usually through another person that he meets our needs. Therefore, it is vital that we serve each other in the kingdom."[17] President Thomas S. Monson, the sixteenth President of the Church, said: "We are surrounded by those in need of our attention, our encouragement, our support, our comfort, our kindness. . . . We are the Lord's hands here upon the earth, with the mandate to serve and to lift His children. He is dependent upon each of us."[18]

Visiting Teaching Today: A Continuing Effort to Follow Jesus Christ

The story of visiting teaching continues in the lives of sisters everywhere, as Latter-day Saint women fulfill their covenant to follow Jesus Christ. President Dieter F. Uchtdorf, a counselor in the First Presidency, said: "You wonderful sisters render compassionate service to others for reasons that supersede desires for personal benefits. In this you emulate the Savior, who, though a king, did not seek position, nor was He concerned about whether others noticed Him. He did not bother to compete with others. His thoughts were always tuned to help others. He taught, healed, conversed [with], and listened to others. He knew that greatness had little to do with outward signs of prosperity or position. He taught and lived by this doctrine: 'He that is greatest among you shall be your servant.'"[19]

Through the years, sisters have learned that visiting teaching requires commitment, dedication, and sacrifice. They have learned that they need the Spirit to direct their visits. They have seen the power that comes through teaching truth and bearing testimony, giving temporal help with love, and being willing to mourn with, comfort, and help bear the burdens of their sisters.

Commitment, Dedication, and Sacrifice

President Kimball emphasized that visiting teachers need complete commitment and dedication. He said: "Your duties in many ways must be much like those of the [home] teachers, which briefly are 'to watch over the church always'—not twenty minutes a month but always—'and be with and strengthen them'—not a knock at the door, but to be with them, and lift them, and strengthen them, and empower them, and fortify them—'and see that there is no iniquity, . . . neither hardness, . . . backbiting, nor evil speaking.' "[20] President Kimball saw such dedication in his wife, Camilla, who

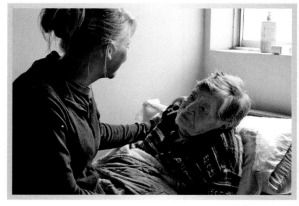

In rendering compassionate service, Relief Society sisters follow the example of Jesus Christ.

"Who, even in the wildest stretch of imagination, can fathom the uncountable acts of charity that have been performed, the food that has been put on barren tables, the faith that has been nurtured in desperate hours of illness, the wounds that have been bound up, the pains that have been ameliorated by loving hands and quiet and reassuring words, the comfort that has been extended in times of death and consequent loneliness?"

Gordon B. Hinckley
Ensign, *Mar. 1992, 4*

Visiting teachers and those they serve can strengthen and uplift one another.

said the following about her efforts as a visiting teacher: "I have tried not to suppress any inclination to generous word or deed."[21]

Visiting teaching is an ongoing assignment; it is never really completed. Visiting teachers often are required to sacrifice and rise above discouragement. This is especially true when their efforts seem to be going nowhere, as in the story of Cathie Humphrey:

"When I was first called to be a visiting teacher, I was assigned a young woman who never came to church. . . . I faithfully went every month and knocked on her door. She would open the inside door but leave the screen door shut. . . . She would not say anything. She would just stand there. I would look cheerful and say, 'Hi, I'm Cathie, your visiting teacher.' And as she would say nothing, I would say, 'Well, our lesson today is on . . .' and try briefly to say something uplifting and friendly. When I was through, she would say, 'Thank you,' and shut the door.

"I did not like going there. . . . But I went because I wanted to be obedient. After about seven or eight months of this, I got a phone call from the bishop.

"'Cathie,' he said, 'the young woman you visit teach just had a baby who lived only a few days. She and her husband are going to have a graveside service, and she asked me to see if you would come and be there with her. She said you are her only friend.' I went to the cemetery. The young woman, her husband, the bishop, and I were at the graveside. That was all.

"I had seen her only once a month for a few minutes at a time. I hadn't even been able to tell through the screen door that she was expecting a baby, yet even my inept but hopeful visiting had blessed us both."[22]

Seeking Spiritual Guidance

Time after time, faithful visiting teachers have sought and received spiritual guidance. A Relief Society sister in Brazil told of a time when she received the Lord's help:

"I have no way to reach the sisters by phone. We don't have telephones. So I go to my knees in prayer to find out the sisters that need me that week. It never fails. [For instance], we had a dear young woman in our ward that had no clothes for her new baby. I had no idea when she was due but I knew she was close. I got a group of sisters together and we made some clothes for her baby. We didn't want her to bring that baby home in newspapers. We could not telephone one another and so I prayed and

I was told when I should go to the hospital with this layette [baby clothes]. When I arrived at the hospital she had just given birth to her baby and I was able to present the clothes to her that were from her Relief Society sisters."[23]

Since each sister's circumstances are different, visiting teachers need specific guidance from the Holy Ghost so they can know how best to help each one. Florence Chukwurah of Nigeria received such guidance when she "was assigned to visit teach a sister who was having difficulties in her marriage and in her home, making it necessary to meet at the marketplace for a visit. After listening to and observing this sister's challenges, Sister Chukwurah asked her husband for a priesthood blessing so that she might know how to help this troubled sister. Following the blessing she felt prompted to discuss with this sister the importance of tithing. 'She tearfully told me that she did not pay her tithes because she was not making enough money,' Sister Chukwurah remember[ed]. 'I suggested that she and I discuss Malachi 3:10 and that we do so in my house so we could relax and be alone for the discussion. She consented. After our discussion I encouraged her to exercise her faith and pay her tithes for at least six months. I bore my testimony to her by the Spirit.'

". . . Within a few months of this meeting, this sister's circumstances changed dramatically.

Her daughter received a scholarship to complete her high school education, her husband worked with the bishop to become active and accept a calling, husband and wife teamed up to improve their financial situation and their relationship, and eventually they became an inspiration to others."[24]

Teaching Truths and Bearing Testimony

President Kimball taught that when visiting teachers share the gospel and their testimonies, they can help their sisters follow the Savior:

"How glorious is the privilege of two sisters going into a home. . . .

"There can be no force in this program as I see it. It is a matter of encouragement and love. It is amazing how many people we can convert with love and inspire with love. We are 'to warn, expound, exhort, and teach, and invite . . . to come unto Christ' (D&C 20:59), as the Lord said in his revelations. . . .

"Don't let us be satisfied with just visits, with making friends; that, of course, has its place. . . . Friendship, of course, is important, but how better can you make a friend than to teach somebody everlasting principles of life and salvation? . . .

"Your testimony is a terrific medium. . . . You don't always have to bear it in the most formal manner; there are so many approaches. . . .

". . . Visiting teachers . . . must excel in energy, and vision, and thoroughness—and in testimony."[25]

A young mother expressed her gratitude for visiting teachers who helped her return to gospel living:

"I'm grateful to this day for my visiting teachers because they loved me and they didn't judge me. They really made me feel as though I really was important and that I did have a place in the Church.

"They'd come over to my home and we would sit and we'd visit . . . , and they would leave me a message each month.

"And when they came every month, it made me feel as if I really did matter and as though they really did care about me and as though they really loved me and appreciated me.

As visiting teachers share truths and bear testimony, they help others follow the Savior.

"Through their visiting and coming to see us, I decided that it was time for me to go back to church. I guess I just really didn't know how to come back, and by their coming and reaching out to me, they provided a way that I could return.

"We need to realize that the Lord loves us no matter who we are, and my visiting teachers helped me see that this was right.

"Now my husband and I have been sealed in the temple."[26]

Visiting teaching is a way to bring the gospel of Jesus Christ into the lives of sisters and their families. Sister Mary Ellen Smoot, the thirteenth Relief Society general president, declared: "My desire is to plead with our sisters to stop worrying about a phone call or a quarterly or monthly visit, and whether that will do, and concentrate instead on nurturing tender souls. Our responsibility is to see that the gospel flame continues to burn brightly. Our charge is to find the lost sheep and help them feel our Savior's love."[27]

President Kimball taught:

"There are many sisters who are living in rags—spiritual rags. They are entitled to gorgeous robes, spiritual robes. . . . It is your privilege to go into homes and exchange robes for rags. . . .

". . . You are going to save souls, and who can tell but that many of the fine active people in

Visiting teachers can receive guidance from the Holy Ghost as they pray for help.

the Church today are active because you were in their homes and gave them a new outlook, a new vision. You pulled back the curtain. You extended their horizons. . . .

"You see, you are not only saving these sisters, but perhaps also their husbands and their homes."[28]

Giving Temporal Help with Love

Charity is at the root of the temporal service and watchcare given by visiting teachers. Often a sister and her family members have physical needs that are difficult or impossible for them to handle alone. This might happen when a baby is born or when illness or death comes to a family member. Like the early Relief Society sisters in Nauvoo and on the trek west to the Salt Lake Valley, modern-day visiting teachers are often the first ones to help. A sister named Veara Fife received such assistance when doctors determined that her legs would have to be amputated:

"She determined not to become a burden to others. Her family encouraged her as she learned to manage in a wheelchair, but they worried about her housework and meal preparation.

"One day her daughter, Norda Emmett, came to help and discovered that the visiting teachers had been there. They had tidied the house; it was spotless. Sister Fife's voice was cheerful, and she was emotionally sustained. Her daughter was embarrassed to have the visiting teachers do the work. She explained to her mother that the family would hire a cleaning woman—the visiting teachers were not to help.

"As her daughter talked with the visiting teachers, they understood the family's feelings. Then they explained how much they had enjoyed their visit with Sister Fife in her home. Her positive attitude had lifted their sights, and she had helped them, in turn, with their genealogy. 'Please don't deny us these blessings,' the visiting teachers said."[29]

Sister Fife's visiting teachers expressed their love through physical labor that she could not do for herself. And they were all strengthened emotionally and spiritually as they served each other.

MARY ELLEN SMOOT
Thirteenth Relief Society General President

"We need each other. We need visiting teachers . . . who are sincerely interested in those they visit and realize the importance of their calling as they strive to reach the one."

Mary Ellen Smoot

Ensign, Feb. 2002, 47

Dedicated visiting teachers practice "pure religion" (James 1:27).

Mourning with Those Who Mourn, Comforting, and Helping to Bear Burdens

Sister Elaine L. Jack, the twelfth Relief Society general president, taught: "In visiting teaching we reach out to each other. Hands often speak as voices can't. A warm embrace conveys volumes. A laugh together unites us. A moment of sharing refreshes our souls. We cannot always lift the burden of one who is troubled, but we can lift her so she can bear it well."[30]

A sister who had recently been widowed was grateful for visiting teachers who mourned with her and comforted her. She wrote: "I was in desperate need of someone to whom I could reach out; someone who would listen to me. . . . And they listened. They comforted me. They wept with me. And they hugged me . . . [and]

"[We are] to feed the hungry, to clothe the naked, to provide for the widow, to dry up the tear of the orphan, to comfort the afflicted, whether in this church, or in any other, or in no church at all, wherever [we find] them."

Joseph Smith

Teachings of Presidents of the Church: Joseph Smith (2007), 426

Through visiting teaching, Relief Society sisters know they have friends who care about them.

convey a sense that she is needed, that someone loves and thinks about her. But equally important is the way the visiting teacher is able to grow in charity. By assigning our women to do visiting teaching, we give them the opportunity to develop the pure love of Christ, which can be the greatest blessing of their lives."[33]

One sister told of blessings that were poured upon her as she served her sisters:

"Shortly after we were married, my husband and I moved to New Jersey. As a first-year medical student, my husband rarely returned home before 11:30 p.m. . . . I hadn't made friends quickly. This move had been lonely and difficult for me.

helped me out of the deep despair and depression of those first months of loneliness."[31]

Another woman summed up her feelings when she was the recipient of true charity from a visiting teacher: "I knew that I was more than just a number on the record books for her to visit. I knew that she cared about me."[32]

"The bishop of my new ward asked me to head up a program for our ward's Spanish-speaking members. This meant translating in sacrament meeting, teaching the gospel doctrine class, and overseeing the Relief Society. Outside of the native Spanish speakers, I was the only woman in the ward who spoke Spanish fluently.

How Visiting Teaching Blesses the Visiting Teacher

When sisters serve others as visiting teachers, they receive blessings themselves. Sister Barbara W. Winder, the eleventh Relief Society general president, taught: "It is vital that each sister have visiting teachers—to

"To add to my responsibilities, the Relief Society president gave me a visiting teaching list of 12 sisters who lived in a barrio across town. I'll admit I was not thrilled about my new assignment. I was busy with my other callings, and I was afraid that I wouldn't know how to reach out. . . . But I made some visiting teaching appointments, and before I knew it I was sitting in the Dumez's living room.

" 'You're my visiting teacher?' Sister Dumez asked as she entered the room. 'Welcome to my home. I haven't had a visiting teacher in two years.' She listened intently to the message, we visited, and she thanked me again and again for coming.

"Before I left she called her five children together to sing 'I Am a Child of God' in Spanish. She hugged me and squeezed my hand. . . .

"All of the visits during that first outing went better than I had anticipated. Throughout the following months, as the sisters graciously welcomed me into their homes, I began to look forward to my visits. But I was unprepared for the stories of tragedy and adversity I heard as I got to know these beautiful people better. I decided to at least try to make life more comfortable for these sisters and their families, many of whom struggled financially. I began taking casseroles when I visited. I took the families on outings. I drove them to doctor appointments and grocery stores.

"I quickly forgot about my own loneliness as I served others. The sisters whom I had

Through visiting teaching, Relief Society sisters can find joy in serving one another.

at first considered so different from myself soon became my dear friends. They were loyal, steadfast friends who were grateful for even the slightest thing I did for them. And they anticipated my needs: I regularly received calls and gifts from the heart. One sister crocheted a doily for my table. Another composed a poem for my birthday.

"Yet, after several months in my callings, I was frustrated at my inability to make life safer or more comfortable for my friends. . . .

"One night I felt especially discouraged. I knelt to pray, pleading with the Lord to show me the direction to take. I felt impressed that the Lord wanted me to help these sisters

"When ye are in the service of your fellow beings ye are only in the service of your God" (Mosiah 2:17).

become more self-reliant and serve each other. I'll admit that I was skeptical that persons carrying such tremendous burdens would have the strength required to lift one another, but I knew I needed to follow the prompting.

"I began by reorganizing the visiting teaching program in the Spanish-speaking Relief Society. One of my faithful friends, Sister Moreira, volunteered to visit six of the sisters by herself. My first response was to protest, 'You can't possibly handle that route without a car. It's too far to walk!' But then I remembered my impression to let the sisters serve each other. I put all six sisters on Sister Moreira's new visiting teaching list.

"Upon returning from her marathon visiting teaching course, Sister Moreira called me, filled with the Spirit. . . . Her feet were sore, but the Lord had lightened her load and her heart.

"After a few more visits, Sister Moreira recruited another sister to walk the route with her. . . .

"Once I started looking, I found all sorts of ways to help these sisters help themselves and each other. . . .

"Just at the time when I could see great spiritual growth developing among the members of my ward, I received notice that my husband and I would be moving. . . . I didn't even want to think about leaving my wonderful friends. I yearned to continue serving with them—we had given each other so much. But at least I could see that the cause of the gospel was moving forth mightily in their lives, and they were looking out for one another. I, who had set out grudgingly to labor in the fields, had returned laden with sheaves."[34]

President Lorenzo Snow, the fifth President of the Church, taught that Relief Society sisters

Lorenzo Snow

exemplify pure religion. He said: "The Apostle James said that 'pure religion and unde-filed before God . . . is this: To visit the fatherless and wid-ows in their affliction, and to keep himself unspotted from the world.' Ac-cepting that as true, the members of the Relief Society have most surely exemplified in their lives pure and undefiled religion; for they have ministered to those in affliction, they have thrown their arms of love around the fatherless and the widows, and they have kept them-selves unspotted from the world. I can testify that there are no purer and more God-fearing women in the world than are to be found within the ranks of the Relief Society."[35]

Pure and God-fearing sisters in the ranks of Relief Society have watched over and strength-ened one another from the beginning days in Nauvoo to the present day, through loving and inspired visiting teaching. It is a ministry that is shared one by one, heart to heart.

How Visiting Teachers Love, Watch Over, and Strengthen a Sister

Pray daily for her and her family.

Seek inspiration to know her and her family.

Visit her regularly to learn how she is doing and to comfort and strengthen her.

Stay in frequent contact through visits, phone calls, letters, e-mail, text mes-sages, and simple acts of kindness.

Greet her at Church meetings.

Help her when she has an emergency, illness, or other urgent need.

Teach her the gospel from the scriptures and the visiting teaching messages.

Inspire her by setting a good example.

Report to a Relief Society leader about their service and the sister's spiritual and temporal well-being.

CHAPTER 8

Blessings of the Priesthood for All

An Inseparable Connection with the Priesthood

There is strength and great capacity in the women of this Church. There is leadership and direction, a certain spirit of independence, and yet great satisfaction in being a part of this, the Lord's kingdom, and of working hand in hand with the priesthood to move it forward.

Gordon B. Hinckley

Blessings of the Priesthood for All
An Inseparable Connection with the Priesthood

Through the Prophet Joseph Smith, the priesthood of God has been restored to the earth in its fulness. The priesthood is the eternal power and authority of God by which He blesses, redeems, and exalts His children, bringing to pass "the immortality and eternal life of man."[1]

Heavenly Father's worthy sons are ordained to priesthood offices and are assigned specific duties and responsibilities. They are authorized to act in His name to look after His children and to help them receive ordinances and make and honor covenants. All Heavenly Father's sons and daughters are equally blessed as they draw upon the power of the priesthood.

In a general conference address, Elder Dallin H. Oaks of the Quorum of the Twelve Apostles taught: "While we sometimes refer to priesthood holders as 'the priesthood,' we must never forget that the priesthood is not owned by or embodied in those who hold it. It is held in a sacred trust to be used for the benefit of men, women, and children alike."[2] Elder Oaks then quoted Elder John A. Widtsoe, who also served as a member of the Quorum of the Twelve: "Men have no greater claim than women upon the blessings that issue from the Priesthood and accompany its possession."[3]

"Full Partakers of the Spiritual Blessings of the Priesthood"

Many Latter-day Saint women have borne witness of the blessings of the priesthood in their lives. Sister Elaine L. Jack, the twelfth Relief Society general president, expressed the feelings of other sisters in Relief Society. "I have a firm testimony of the power of the priesthood in the lives of all Church members," she said. "In the Doctrine and Covenants we are . . . told that the Melchizedek Priesthood holds 'the keys of all the spiritual blessings of the church' (D&C 107:18). I know it is God's power and authority on earth to bless our lives and help us bridge our earthly experiences to the eternities. When we receive the blessings of the priesthood, we are drawing on the power and grace of God." Sister Jack continued:

"It is significant to me that the women were organized under the authority of the priesthood. We sustain the priesthood and are sustained by its power. The sisters of the Church . . . treasure our opportunity to be full partakers of the spiritual blessings of the priesthood.

"Each of us can be directed and blessed in our eternal progression by receiving these blessings. The ordinances, covenants, sealings, and the gift of the Holy Ghost are essential for exaltation. There are a host of individual priesthood blessings as well. Priesthood blessings give us direction; they lift our sights; they encourage and inspire us; they prompt our commitment. We can all be partakers of these spiritual blessings."[4]

Sister Sheri L. Dew, who served as a counselor in the general Relief Society presidency, echoed these teachings: "Sisters, some will try to persuade you that because you are not ordained to the priesthood, you have been shortchanged. They are simply wrong, and they do not understand the gospel of Jesus Christ. The blessings of the priesthood are available to every righteous man and woman. We may all receive the Holy Ghost, obtain personal revelation, and be endowed in the temple, from which we emerge 'armed' with power. The power of the priesthood heals, protects, and inoculates all of the righteous against the powers of darkness. Most significantly, the fulness of the priesthood contained in the highest ordinances of the house of the Lord can be received only by a man and woman together."[5]

Ordinances, Covenants, and Blessings

When Joseph Smith organized the Relief Society in Nauvoo, Illinois, in the spring of 1842, its members were women who had already been blessed by some priesthood ordinances and covenants. They had been baptized for the remission of sins. They had received the gift of the Holy Ghost, giving them the right to the constant companionship of the Spirit and the ability to be guided by personal revelation. They had partaken of the sacrament in remembrance of Jesus Christ and their covenants. They had received gifts of the Spirit. Some had received patriarchal blessings, learning of their individual gifts and potential and of their membership in the house of Israel. The Lord had healed them, comforted them, and instructed them according to their needs, their faith, and His will.

Sister Elizabeth Ann Whitney, who attended the first Relief Society meeting, had learned

Elizabeth Ann Whitney

about the restored gospel 12 years earlier, in 1830. "As soon as I heard the Gospel as the Elders preached it," she later said, "I knew it to be the voice of the Good Shepherd." She "was baptized immediately," and her husband, Newel K. Whitney, was baptized a

As Latter-day Saint women make and keep covenants, the Lord strengthens them to serve in His kingdom.

few days later.[6] Recalling this experience, she told of the blessings she received through the priesthood ordinances of baptism and confirmation:

"If there are any principles which have given me strength, and by which I have learned to live more truly a life of usefulness, it seems to me I could wish to impart this joy and strength to others; to tell them what the Gospel has been and is to me, ever since I embraced it and learned to live by its laws. A fresh revelation of the Spirit day by day, an unveiling of mysteries which before were dark, deep, unexplained and incomprehensible; a most implicit faith in a divine power, in infinite truth emanating from God the Father."[7]

"When you attend the temple and perform the ordinances that pertain to the House of the Lord, certain blessings will come to you. . . . You will receive the key of the knowledge of God. (See D&C 84:19.) You will learn how you can be like Him. Even the power of godliness will be manifest to you. (See D&C 84:20.)"

Ezra Taft Benson
Ensign, *Aug. 1985, 10*

Gifts of the Spirit

On April 28, 1842, Joseph Smith spoke at a meeting of the Female Relief Society of Nauvoo. Part of his discourse was based on the Apostle Paul's teachings in 1 Corinthians 12–13 about the gifts of the Spirit. Joseph Smith emphasized that "these signs, such as healing the sick, casting out devils etc. should follow all that believe."[8]

Because Latter-day Saint women have received the gift of the Holy Ghost, they can seek and be blessed by spiritual gifts such as "the gift of tongues, prophecy, revelation, visions, healing, interpretation of tongues, and so forth."[9] Throughout the history of the Church, Latter-day Saint women have received gifts of the Spirit and used them to bless their families and others.

Amanda Barnes Smith was present on April 28, 1842, when Joseph Smith taught Relief Society sisters about gifts of the Spirit. She knew the truth of his teachings, for she had been blessed with the gift of revelation about four years earlier at a time when she needed the Lord's help to save her son.

In late October 1838, Amanda and her husband, Warren, with their children and other members of the Church, were on the way to Far West, Missouri. They stopped at a mill to make some repairs on their wagon. While they were there, a mob attacked Latter-day Saints who

Amanda Smith prayed for help to care for her son.

were working at the mill, killing 17 men and boys and wounding 15. Amanda, who had hidden during the attack, returned to find Warren and their son Sardius among the dead. Another son, Alma, was severely wounded. His hip had been blown off by a gun blast. Amanda later told of the personal revelation she received so her son could be healed:

"I [was] there, all that long, dreadful night, with my dead and my wounded, and none but God as our physician and help.

"Oh my Heavenly Father, I cried, what shall I do? Thou seest my poor wounded boy and knowest my inexperience. Oh Heavenly Father direct me what to do!

"And then I was directed as by a voice speaking to me."

Amanda was directed to make a lye, or washing solution, from the ashes of their fire to clean the wound. Then she was directed to make a poultice out of cloth and slippery elm to fill the wound. The next day she found some balsam and poured it into the wound to soothe Alma's pain.

"'Alma, my child,' I said, 'you believe that the Lord made your hip?'

"'Yes, mother.'

"'Well, the Lord can make something there in the place of your hip, don't you believe he can, Alma?'

"'Do you think that the Lord can, mother?' inquired the child, in his simplicity.

"'Yes, my son,' I replied, 'he has shown it all to me in a vision.'

"Then I laid him comfortably on his face, and said: 'Now you lay like that, and don't move, and the Lord will make you another hip.'

"So Alma laid on his face for five weeks, until he was entirely recovered—a flexible gristle having grown in place of the missing joint and socket, . . . a marvel to physicians.

"On the day that he walked again I was out of the house fetching a bucket of water, when I heard screams from the children. Running back, in affright, I entered, and there was Alma on the floor, dancing around, and the children screaming in astonishment and joy."[10]

Through the spiritual gift of revelation, the Lord taught Sister Smith how to care for her son. She, like Elizabeth Ann Whitney and countless others, received "joy and strength" and "fresh revelation of the Spirit"[11] because of her faithfulness.

Temple Blessings

One of the Lord's purposes in organizing the Relief Society was to prepare His daughters for the greater blessings of the priesthood found in the ordinances and covenants of the temple. The early sisters in Nauvoo anticipated the completion of the temple with great excitement, for they knew, as the Prophet Joseph Smith

Nauvoo Illinois Temple

Temple ordinance workers on the steps of the Salt Lake Temple, 1917

promised Mercy Fielding Thompson, that the endowment would bring them "out of darkness into marvelous light."[12]

Through the Prophet Joseph Smith, the Lord revealed the following to Latter-day Saints in Kirtland, Ohio: "I gave unto you a commandment that you should build a house, in the which house I design to endow those whom I have chosen with power from on high."[13] He promised to give faithful Saints a "multiplicity of blessings,"[14] and He declared that the temple would be "a place of thanksgiving for all saints, and . . . a place of instruction for all those who are called to the work of the ministry in all their several callings and offices; that they may be perfected in the understanding of their ministry, in theory, in principle, and in doctrine, in all things pertaining to the kingdom of God on the earth."[15]

In Nauvoo, the Lord again commanded the Saints to build a temple, saying that He would restore the "fulness of the priesthood" and "reveal [His] ordinances" there.[16]

Relief Society sisters helped each other prepare for these ordinances and their attendant covenants. They contributed to the building of the temple, learned from the Prophet and from each other in Relief Society meetings, charitably served one another, and sought to live with greater sanctity.

As the temple neared completion, 36 women were called to serve as temple ordinance workers. Elizabeth Ann Whitney, one of those first ordinance workers, recalled: "I gave myself, my time and attention to that mission. I worked in the Temple every day without cessation until it was closed."[17]

In the ordinances of the higher priesthood that the Saints received in the Nauvoo Temple, "the power of godliness [was] manifest."[18] As the Saints kept their covenants, this power strengthened and sustained them through their trials in the days and years ahead (see chapter 3).

In the Church today, faithful women and men all over the world continue to serve in the temple and

Joseph Fielding Smith

find strength in the blessings that can be received only through temple ordinances. As President Joseph Fielding Smith, the tenth President of the Church, stated, "It is within the privilege of the sisters of this Church to receive exaltation in the kingdom of God and receive authority and power as queens and priestesses."[19]

"The only place on earth where we can receive the fulness of the blessings of the priesthood is in the holy temple. That is the only place where, through holy ordinances, we can receive that which will qualify us for exaltation in the celestial kingdom."

Harold B. Lee

Stand Ye in Holy Places
(1974), 117

Priesthood in the Home

Relief Society helps sisters strengthen homes and families, thus helping to accomplish one of the fundamental purposes of the priesthood. "Priesthood authority has been restored," said Elder Russell M. Nelson of the Quorum of the Twelve Apostles, "so that families can be sealed eternally."[20] Elder Richard G. Scott, also of the Quorum of the Twelve, taught: "The family and the home are the foundation of the righteous life. The priesthood is the power and the priesthood line is the means provided by the Lord to support the family."[21] Relief Society assists in this work by helping women and their families live the gospel in such a way that they can receive promised blessings of the priesthood.

Husband and Wife

Elder Dallin H. Oaks of the Quorum of the Twelve Apostles said: "The ultimate and highest expression of womanhood and manhood is in the new and everlasting covenant of marriage between a man and a woman. Only this relationship culminates in exaltation. As the Apostle Paul taught, 'Neither is the man without the woman, neither the woman without the man, in the Lord.'"[22] Ancient scripture confirms this in the accounts of covenant marriages between Abraham and Sarah, Isaac and Rebekah, and Jacob and Rachel. The sealing ordinance binds husband and wife to each other, to their children, and to their Father in Heaven. "Thus," continued Elder Oaks, "the common objective . . . in our priesthood quorums and . . . in our Relief Societies is to bring men and women together in the sacred marriage and family relationships that lead toward eternal life, 'the greatest of all the gifts of God.'"[23]

When a husband and wife are blessed with the opportunity to be parents, they share a solemn responsibility to help their children understand and receive priesthood ordinances and covenants.[24] Our first parents, Adam and Eve, set an example of an interdependent and unified relationship when they taught their children. Elder Bruce R. McConkie of the Quorum of the Twelve Apostles taught:

"It was not Adam alone, who was involved in these things. . . .

"Eve was an active participant. She heard all that Adam said. She spoke of 'our transgression,' of 'the joy of our redemption,' of the 'seed' they should have together, and of the 'eternal life' which could not come to either of them alone, but which is always reserved for a man and a woman together.

"She and Adam both prayed; they both blessed the name of the Lord; they both taught their children; they both received revelation; and the Lord commanded both of them to worship and serve him in the name of Jesus Christ forever."[25]

Latter-day prophets and apostles have encouraged husbands and wives to follow this pattern in their homes: "By divine design, fathers are to preside over their families in love and righteousness and are responsible to provide the necessities of life and protection for their families. Mothers are primarily responsible for the nurture of their children. In these sacred responsibilities, fathers and mothers are

Adam and Eve had a unified covenant relationship.

obligated to help one another as equal partners. Disability, death, or other circumstances may necessitate individual adaptation. Extended families should lend support when needed."[26]

Latter-day Saints all over the world follow this counsel in simple but powerful ways. Husbands and wives gather their children to pray and read the scriptures. In many homes, parents establish a special place—perhaps a simple shelf—where they keep scriptures and other Church resources. They teach the gospel through their words and their examples. They help their children prepare to receive the blessings of the temple, serve full-time missions, establish homes of their own, and continue serving in the Church. Like Adam and Eve,

they share the responsibilities to teach, to pray, to serve, and to worship the Lord.

In some cases, a husband or wife may feel alone in these responsibilities because their spouse has not made covenants or has strayed from covenants that have been made. Even in these situations, faithful family members need not feel alone. They are blessed and strengthened through the priesthood ordinances they have received and the covenants they keep. They can also call upon the support of extended family members and other Latter-day Saints.

Single Sisters and the Priesthood

Many Latter-day Saints have never been married. Others are single because of the

BARBARA B. SMITH
Tenth Relief Society General President

"With continuing priesthood counsel and with Relief Society leaders who are called of the Lord by inspiration, the women of the Church have a divine source of direction for the work that is theirs to do, and the Society provides a means to accomplish that work."

Barbara B. Smith

Ensign, *Mar. 1983, 23*

Relief Society supports women as they nurture their children.

death of a spouse, abandonment, or divorce. Like all members of the Church, these members will be blessed as they remain faithful to their covenants and do all they can to strive for the ideal of living in an eternal family. They can enjoy the blessings, strength, and influence of the priesthood in their lives and homes through the ordinances they have received and the covenants they keep.

Elder Dallin H. Oaks told of the faithfulness of his mother, who was widowed at a young age. Having been sealed to her husband in the temple, she did not consider herself single; nevertheless, she had to rear her three children alone. Elder Oaks recalled:

"My father died when I was seven. I was the oldest of three small children our widowed mother struggled to raise. When I was ordained a deacon, she said how pleased she was to have a priesthood holder in the home. But Mother continued to direct the family, including calling on which one of us would pray when we knelt together each morning. . . .

"When my father died, my mother presided over our family. She had no priesthood office, but as the surviving parent in her marriage she had become the governing officer in her family. At the same time, she was always totally respectful of the priesthood authority of our bishop and other Church leaders. She presided over her family, but they presided over the Church. . . .

"The faithful widowed mother who raised us had no confusion about the eternal nature of the family. She always honored the position of our deceased father. She made him a presence in our home. She spoke of the eternal duration of their temple marriage. She often reminded us of what our father would like us to do so we could realize the Savior's promise that we could be a family forever."[27]

Another man told of his mother presiding in the home: "Just as I was preparing to serve a full-time mission, my father left our family and the Church. Under these circumstances, it was difficult for me to leave home for two years, but I went. And while I served the Lord in a faraway land, I learned of my mother's strength at home. She needed and appreciated the special attention she received from men who held the priesthood—her father and brothers, her home teachers, other men in the ward. However, her greatest strength came from the Lord Himself. She did not have to wait for a visit in order to have the blessings of the priesthood in her home, and when visitors left, those blessings did not leave with them. Because she was faithful to the covenants she had made in the waters of baptism and in the temple, she always had the blessings of the priesthood in her life. The Lord gave her inspiration and strength beyond her own capacity, and she raised children who now keep the same covenants that have sustained her."[28]

These women understood that they received added strength and help through the covenants they had made and kept.

Serving in the Church

All those who serve in an official capacity in The Church of Jesus Christ of Latter-day Saints do so under the direction and authority of those who hold priesthood keys, such as bishops and stake presidents. In Relief Society, this pattern was established in the first Relief Society meeting. As instructed by the Prophet Joseph Smith, Elder John Taylor of the Quorum of the Twelve Apostles laid his hands on the heads of Sister Emma Smith and her counselors, Sisters Sarah M. Cleveland and Elizabeth Ann Whitney, one by one. He blessed them to be guided in their service. Ever since, sisters who have served in Relief Society callings, in all other Church callings, and as visiting teachers have served under the authority of those who hold priesthood keys.

President Boyd K. Packer of the Quorum of the Twelve Apostles stated:

"The Relief Society works under the direction of the Melchizedek Priesthood, for 'all other authorities or offices in the church are appendages to this priesthood.' It was organized 'after the pattern of the priesthood.' . . .

"The Brethren know they *belong* to a quorum of the priesthood. Too many sisters, however, think that Relief Society is merely a class to attend. The same sense of *belonging* to the Relief Society rather than just attending a class must be fostered in the heart of every woman."[29]

Priesthood quorums organize men in a brotherhood to give service, to learn and carry out their duties, and to study the doctrines of the gospel. Relief Society accomplishes these same purposes for the women of the Church. All women in the Church belong to Relief Society, even if they have other responsibilities that make it difficult for them to attend all Relief Society meetings. They continue to be watched over and taught through the sisterhood of Relief Society.

Unity: "All Must Act in Concert"

In The Church of Jesus Christ of Latter-day Saints, men and women are to strengthen and fortify one another and work together in unity. The Lord said, "Be one; and if ye are not one ye are not mine."[30]

The Prophet Joseph Smith taught, "All must act in concert or nothing can be done."[31] And he set an example by working in concert with others. Sister Eliza R. Snow remembered and cherished this example all her life. She shared it with local Church leaders when the

A sense of belonging to the Relief Society "must be fostered in the heart of every woman" (Boyd K. Packer).

"I pray that [a] spirit of oneness may spread throughout all the Church, that it may be characteristic of Presidencies of Stakes and High Councils, Bishoprics, [Home Teachers], and particularly of the quorums and auxiliaries of the Church, that they may all be one, to quote the Savior, as he and his Father are one."

David O. McKay

In Conference Report, Apr. 1937, 121–22; referring to John 17:21

Relief Society was reestablished in Utah. She taught that bishops were to "have the same relation" with ward Relief Societies as Joseph Smith did with the Relief Society in Nauvoo. She also taught that "each society . . . could not exist without [the bishop's] counsel." [32]

When Sister Bathsheba W. Smith served as the fourth Relief Society general president, she remembered Joseph Smith's teachings and example. She instructed Relief Society sisters to work in harmony with priesthood leaders. She said: "We humbly desire to magnify the callings given to us of the Lord, and in order to do so acceptably, we shall need the faith and support of the First Presidency of the Church, the Apostles, presidents of Stakes and Bishops, whom we ever feel to uphold, and with whom we desire to work in harmony." [33]

This pattern has endured through the decades. President Henry B. Eyring, a counselor in the First Presidency, said, "A wonderful part of the heritage of Relief Society is evident in the way the priesthood has always shown respect to and received it from the Relief Society in turn." [34]

When Sister Barbara W. Winder began her service as the eleventh Relief Society general president, President Gordon B. Hinckley, who was then serving as a counselor in the First Presidency, asked her to unite the sisters who served in Relief Society, Young Women, and Primary under the priesthood. Sister Winder

BARBARA W. WINDER
Eleventh Relief Society General President

"I want so, and desire so, that we be unified, one together with the priesthood, serving and building the kingdom of God here today and spreading the joy of the gospel to those who are so in need of it. This is His kingdom. We have a great responsibility to share it."

Barbara W. Winder

In Conference Report, Apr. 1984, 79; or Ensign, May 1984, 59

realized that unity is "not simply a matter of the sisters working together, but that we are partners with the priesthood brethren. We are companions in the work."[35]

Sister Winder said that shortly after she was called to serve as Relief Society general president, Elder Dallin H. Oaks asked to meet with her. He had been asked to prepare a statement for the Church on an important issue, and he felt that he must have input from the female leaders of the Church. He showed respect and gratitude for Sister Winder's knowledge, opinions, and inspiration by asking for and using her help.

Sister Winder later taught that men and women in the Church need each other's help in the work. "I learned that when you are invited to a meeting," she explained, "you are not invited to come and complain about all your problems, but you are invited to come with solutions. Then together you can talk about ideas to see what will work. The priesthood brethren expect and need the perspective of the women of the Church. We need to be prepared and assist them."[36]

This unity of purpose is evident in the council meetings of the Church. As the men and women on these councils listen to one another, seek the guidance of the Spirit, and work in unity, they receive inspiration to know how to meet the needs of individuals and families. The

In the Church, men and women work together in unity.

Lord has said, "Where two or three are gathered together in my name, as touching one thing, behold, there will I be in the midst of them."[37]

President Thomas S. Monson, the sixteenth President of the Church, shared an example of what can happen when Relief Society sisters and priesthood brethren work together in the Lord's service:

"On August 24, [1992,] Hurricane Andrew slammed into the Florida coast south of Miami. Wind gusts exceeded two hundred miles per hour. . . . Eighty-seven thousand homes were destroyed, leaving 150,000 homeless. . . .

"Local priesthood and Relief Society leaders organized rapidly to assess injuries and damage and to assist in the cleanup effort. Three large waves of member volunteers, numbering over five thousand, labored shoulder to shoulder with disaster-stricken residents, helping to repair three thousand homes, a Jewish synagogue, a Pentecostal church, and two schools."[38]

"Hand in Hand with the Priesthood": Inspired Counsel from Latter-day Prophets

Latter-day prophets have spoken of the blessings that come to the Church and to families when faithful priesthood brethren and faithful Relief Society sisters work together.

President Spencer W. Kimball, the twelfth President of the Church, said, "There is a power in this organization [of Relief Society] that has not yet been fully exercised to strengthen the homes of Zion and build the Kingdom of God—nor will it until both the sisters and the priesthood catch the vision of Relief Society."[39]

President Joseph Fielding Smith summarized the relationship between the Relief Society and priesthood quorums:

"They [the sisters] have their own meetings, such as the Relief Society, in which they have been given power and authority to do a great many things. . . .

"The Lord through his wisdom has called upon our sisters to be aids to the Priesthood. Because of their sympathy, tenderness of heart, and kindness, the Lord looks upon them and

"There is strength and great capacity in the women of this Church" (Gordon B. Hinckley).

gives unto them the duties and responsibilities of being ministers to the needy and to the afflicted. He has pointed out the path which they should follow, and he has given to them this great organization where they have authority to serve under the directions of the bishops of the wards and in harmony with the bishops of the wards, looking after the interest of our people both spiritually and temporally."[40]

When President Gordon B. Hinckley was serving as the fifteenth President of the Church, he shared the following with Relief Society sisters:

"Let me say to you sisters that you do not hold a second place in our Father's plan for the eternal happiness and well-being of His children. You are an absolutely essential part of that plan.

"Without you the plan could not function. Without you the entire program would be frustrated. . . .

"Each of you is a daughter of God, endowed with a divine birthright. You need no defense of that position. . . .

". . . There is strength and great capacity in the women of this Church. There is leadership and direction, a certain spirit of independence, and yet great satisfaction in being a part of this, the Lord's kingdom, and of working hand in hand with the priesthood to move it forward."[41]

"Guardians of the Hearth"

Establishing, Nurturing, and Defending the Family

To be a righteous woman during the winding up scenes on this earth, before the second coming of our Savior, is an especially noble calling. . . . She has been placed here to help to enrich, to protect, and to guard the home—which is society's basic and most noble institution.

Spencer W. Kimball

O LE AIG...

O SE FOLAFOLAG...
LALOLAG...

O Le Au Peresitene Sili ma le Aufono a Apo...
O Le Ekalesia a Iesu Keriso o le Au Pai...

O I MATOU, O LE AU PERESITENE SILI ma le Aufono a
Aposetolo e Toasefululua O Le Ekalesia a Iesu Keriso o le Au
Paia o le Aso e Gata Ai, matou te ta'utino atu ma le faamaoni,
o le faaipoipoga i le va o se alii ma se tamaitai, ua faauina e
le Atua, ma o le aiga o le totonugalemu lea o le fuafuaga a Lē
Foafoa, mo le taunuuga e faavavau o Lana fanau.

O TAGATA UMA—tane ma le fafine—ua foafoaina i le faatusa
o le Atua. O'i latou taitoatasi o se atalii po o se afafine agaga
faapelepele a ni matua faalelagi, ma, o lea ua tofu ai ma se

le Alii" (Salam...
a latou fanau.
mea e man...
latou c...
ma avea...
te nonofo...
atu i le Atu...

O LE AIGA ua...
alii ma le tama...

CHAPTER 9

"Guardians of the Hearth"
Establishing, Nurturing, and Defending the Family

On September 23, 1995, President Gordon B. Hinckley, the fifteenth President of the Church, stood before the women of the Church in a general Relief Society meeting. He expressed gratitude for the faithfulness and diligence of Latter-day Saint women—young and old, married and single, with children and without children. Acknowledging the serious challenges they faced, he offered encouragement, counsel, and warning to help them fulfill their responsibilities and find joy in life. Toward the end of his address, he said:

"With so much of sophistry that is passed off as truth, with so much of deception concerning standards and values, with so much of allurement and enticement to take on the slow stain of the world, we have felt to warn and fore-warn. In furtherance of this we of the First Presidency and the Council of the Twelve Apostles now issue a proclamation to the Church and to the world as a declaration

Gordon B. Hinckley

and reaffirmation of standards, doctrines, and practices relative to the family which the prophets, seers, and revelators of this church have repeatedly stated throughout its history."[1] Then he read "The Family: A Proclamation to the World." This was the first time the proclamation was read publicly.

In the proclamation, the First Presidency and Quorum of the Twelve Apostles declare that "happiness in family life is most likely to be achieved when founded upon the teachings of the Lord Jesus Christ." They "solemnly proclaim that marriage between a man and a woman is ordained of God and that the family is central to the Creator's plan for the eternal destiny of His children." They remind husbands and wives of their "solemn responsibility to love and care for each other and for their children."[2]

As the proclamation's title emphasizes, it was published as "A Proclamation to the World"— reminding all people, including the leaders of nations, of the eternal importance of the family.

Eight months after presenting the proclamation, President Hinckley spoke in a press conference in Tokyo, Japan. He said: "Why do we have this proclamation on the family now? Because the family is under attack. All across the world families are falling apart. The place to begin to improve society is in the home. Children do, for the most part, what they are taught. We are trying to make the world better by making the family stronger."[3]

The testimonies of Relief Society sisters show that in addition to being a proclamation to the entire world, this statement of doctrine has meaning for each family and each individual in the Church. The principles in the proclamation have touched the hearts of sisters in all circumstances.

Sister Barbara Thompson, who later was called to serve as a counselor in the Relief  Society general presidency, was in the Salt Lake Tabernacle when President Hinckley read the proclamation there. "That was a great occasion," she recalled. "I felt the significance of the message. I also found myself thinking, 'This is a great guide for parents. It is also a big responsibility for parents.' I thought for a moment that it really didn't pertain too much to me since I wasn't married and didn't have any children.

Barbara Thompson

But almost as quickly I thought, 'But it does pertain to me. I am a member of a family. I am a daughter, a sister, an aunt, a cousin, a niece, and a granddaughter. I do have responsibilities—and blessings—because I am a member of a family. Even if I were the only living member of my family, I am still a member of God's family, and I have a responsibility to help strengthen other families.'"[4]

Sister Bonnie D. Parkin, who later served as the fourteenth Relief Society general president, was also in the Tabernacle when President Hinckley read the proclamation. She recalled: "Stillness was in the congregation but also a sense of excitement, a reaction of 'Yes—we need help with our families!' I remember feeling it was so right. Tears ran down my cheeks. As I looked at the sisters seated near me, they seemed to be experiencing similar feelings. There was so much in the proclamation that I couldn't wait to get a copy and study it. The proclamation affirms the dignity of women. And to think that it was first given to the women of the Church at the general Relief Society meeting."[5]

Why did the First Presidency choose to announce the proclamation on the family in a general Relief Society meeting? After President Hinckley read it, he provided an answer to that question. "You are the guardians of the hearth," he told the sisters. "You are the bearers of the

"Mothers are the heart and soul of any family" (James E. Faust).

children. You are they who nurture them and establish within them the habits of their lives. No other work reaches so close to divinity as does the nurturing of the sons and daughters of God."[6]

President James E. Faust, President Hinckley's second counselor, added the following explanation: "Because you mothers are the heart and soul of any family, it was appropriate that it [the proclamation] was first read in the general Relief Society meeting."[7]

A "Reaffirmation of Standards, Doctrines, and Practices"

The teachings in the family proclamation were not new in 1995. As President Hinckley stated, they were a

"We call upon parents to devote their best efforts to the teaching and rearing of their children in gospel principles which will keep them close to the Church. The home is the basis of a righteous life, and no other instrumentality can take its place or fulfill its essential functions in carrying forward this God-given responsibility."

First Presidency (Gordon B. Hinckley, Thomas S. Monson, James E. Faust)

Ensign, *June 1999, 80*

"reaffirmation of standards, doctrines, and practices."[8] They had been "central to the Creator's plan" even before He created the earth.[9]

Sister Julie B. Beck, the fifteenth Relief Society general president, taught: "In The Church of Jesus Christ of Latter-day Saints, we have a theology of the family that is based on the Creation, the Fall, and the Atonement. The Creation of the earth provided a place where families could live. . . . The Fall provided a way for the family to grow. . . . The Atonement allows for the family to be sealed together eternally."[10]

The sons of the Anti-Nephi-Lehies acquired great faith through the teachings of their mothers (see Alma 56:47).

Faithful women and men have been true to this theology of the family and followed these standards, doctrines, and practices whenever the gospel has been on the earth. "Our glorious Mother Eve" and our "Father Adam" were leaders for their children, teaching them "the joy of our redemption, and the eternal life which God giveth unto all the obedient."[11] Rebekah and Isaac ensured that priesthood covenants and blessings would not be lost for their family.[12] A widow in the city of Zarephath was able to take care of her son because she had faith to follow the prophet Elijah.[13] Two thousand sixty young warriors fought valiantly to protect their families, trusting their mothers' promise that "God would deliver them."[14] As a young man, Jesus Christ "increased in wisdom and stature, and in favour with God and man," nurtured by the love and concern of His mother, Mary, and her husband, Joseph.[15]

With the restoration of the gospel, early members of the Church increased in their understanding of the importance of the family.[16] The Saints learned that by the power of the priesthood, they could receive temple ordinances and covenants that would bind their families together forever. This promise strengthened Latter-day Saints in fulfilling their roles as sons and daughters of God.

Early Relief Society leaders encouraged women to make their families a central focus in their lives. Sister Eliza R. Snow, the second Relief Society general president, never had children of her own. Nevertheless, she recognized the importance of a mother's influence. She counseled Relief Society sisters, "Let your first business be to perform your duties at home."[17] Sister Zina D. H. Young, the third Relief Society general president, taught sisters to "make the home the centre of attraction, where the spirit of love, peace and unity will dwell, and that sweet charity that thinketh no evil will ever abide."[18]

Mary Fielding Smith set an example as a strong, loving mother. Her son Joseph F. Smith, who became the sixth President of the Church, recalled:

"I can remember my mother in the days of Nauvoo. I remember seeing her and her helpless children hustled into a flat boat with such things as she could carry out of the house at the commencement of the bombardment of the city of Nauvoo by the mob. I remember the hardships of the Church there and on the way to Winter Quarters, on the Missouri river, and how she prayed for her children and family on her wearisome journey. . . . I can remember all the trials incident to our endeavors to move out with the Camp of Israel, coming to these valleys of the mountains without teams sufficient to draw our wagons; and being without the means to get those teams necessary, she yoked up her cows and calves, and tied two

Rebekah, here with Abraham's servant, understood the importance of marriage in the covenant (see Genesis 24:1–28).

wagons together, and we started to come to Utah in this crude and helpless condition, and my mother said—'The Lord will open the way;' but how He would open the way no one knew. I was a little boy then, and I drove team and did my share of the work. I remember coming upon her in her secret prayer to God to enable her to accomplish her mission. Do you not think that these things make an impression upon the mind? Do you think I can forget the example of my mother? No; her faith and example will ever be bright in my memory. What do I think! Every breath I breathe, every feeling of my soul rises to God in thankfulness to

Him that my mother was a Saint, that she was a woman of God, pure and faithful, and that she would suffer death rather than betray the trust committed to her; that she would suffer poverty and distress in the wilderness and try to hold her family together rather than remain in Babylon. That is the spirit which imbued her and her children." [19]

Temporal Responsibilities and Eternal Roles

In harmony with timeless principles about the sacred nature of home and family, Melchizedek Priesthood quorums help men fulfill their responsibilities as sons, brothers, husbands, and fathers. The Relief Society helps women fulfill their responsibilities as daughters, sisters, wives, and mothers. Relief Society sisters have always supported one another in efforts to strengthen families, learn practical skills that improve their homes, and make their homes places where the Spirit can dwell.

Nurturing Families

Sister Zina D. H. Young was a loving, nurturing mother, and she taught Relief Society sisters the principles that guided her own efforts at home. She counseled: "If there is one mother present here who does not teach and instruct her children properly, . . . I plead with you to do so. Call your children around you

BONNIE D. PARKIN
Fourteenth Relief Society General President

"*If I could have one thing happen for parents and leaders of this Church, it would be that they feel the love of the Lord in their lives each day as they care for Heavenly Father's children. . . . I invite you, in all of your dealings, to put on the mantle of charity, to envelop your family in the pure love of Christ.*"

Bonnie D. Parkin

Ensign, *June 2006, 93, 97*

. . . and pray with them. . . . Warn the children of the evils that surround us . . . that they may not become a prey to these evils, but grow up in holiness and in purity before the Lord."[20] She also taught: "Be diligent in all the duties of life, as mothers and wives. . . . Let us be careful to speak with wisdom before our little ones, avoiding fault-finding, . . . and cultivate the higher attributes of our nature, that will tend to elevate, refine and purify the heart. . . . We should take the utmost pains to teach the children of Zion to be honest, virtuous, upright and punctual in all their duties; also to be industrious and keep the Sabbath day holy. . . . Mothers should never speak a word detrimental to the father's best interest before the children, for they are close observers. Sow good seeds in their young and tender minds, and always prefer principle to policy, thus you will lay up treasures in heaven."[21]

When Sister Bathsheba W. Smith served as the fourth Relief Society general president, she saw a need to strengthen families, and so she established mother education lessons for Relief Society sisters. The lessons included counsel on marriage, prenatal care, and child rearing. These lessons supported President Joseph F. Smith's teachings about the Relief Society helping women in their roles at home:

"Wherever there is ignorance or at least a lack of understanding in regard to the family, duties of the family, with regard to obligations that should exist and that do rightfully exist between husband and wife and between parents and children, there this organization exists or is near at hand, and by the natural endowments and inspiration that belongs to the organization they are prepared and ready to impart instruction with reference to those important duties. Where there is a young mother, that has not had the experience that she should have to nurture and nurse her child, or to make her home pleasant and attractive and desirable for herself and her husband, this organization

The Relief Society helps mothers in their sacred responsibilities.

Mothers and grandmothers can prepare their daughters and granddaughters to be nurturers.

exists, in some part of its organization, to impart instruction to that young mother, and to help her to do her duty and to do it well. And wherever there is lack of experience in administering natural and nourishing and proper food to children, or where there is a necessity of giving proper spiritual instruction and spiritual food to children, there are in the great organizations of the Female Relief Societies of the Church of Jesus Christ of Latter-day Saints and organizations of mothers and daughters of Zion, those who are equipped to impart that instruction."[22]

The ability to nurture is not confined to women who have children of their own. Sister Sheri L. Dew observed: "For reasons known to the Lord, some women are required to wait to have children. This delay is not easy for any righteous woman. But the Lord's timetable for each of us does not negate our nature. Some of us, then, must simply find other ways to mother. And all around us are those who need to be loved and led."[23]

Sisters in the Church have opportunities to nurture when they receive callings as leaders and teachers and when they serve as visiting teachers. Some sisters provide motherly love and in-fluence for children who were not born to them. Single sisters have often been at the forefront of such efforts, blessing the lives of children who need the influence of righteous women. Sometimes this nurturing has contin-ued for days, weeks, and years. Through selfless service and personal faith, women have rescued many children from emotional, spiritual, and physical danger.

Making Home a Center of Strength

Since the early days of Relief Society in Nauvoo, Illinois, sisters have gathered to learn about their charitable and practical responsibilities. They have practiced skills to help them increase faith and personal righteousness, strengthen their families and make their homes centers of spiritual strength, and help those in need. They have applied principles of provident living and spiritual and temporal self-reliance. They have also increased in sisterhood and unity as they have taught one another and served together. This training has blessed sisters in all circumstances. Sister Bonnie D. Parkin told about how these meetings strengthened her:

"As members of the Relief Society of The Church of Jesus Christ of Latter-day Saints, it is our blessing and our responsibility to nurture and sustain the family unit. Everyone belongs to a family, and every family needs to be strengthened and protected.

"My greatest help in becoming a homemaker came first from my own mother and grandmother and next from the Relief Society sisters in the different wards where we have lived. I learned skills; I saw modeled the

"Whenever . . . temptations became most alluring and most tempting to me, the first thought that arose in my soul was this: Remember the love of your mother. Remember how she strove for your welfare. Remember how willing she was to sacrifice her life for your good. Remember what she taught you in your childhood. . . . This feeling toward my mother became a defense, a barrier between me and temptation."

Joseph F. Smith

Teachings of Presidents of the Church: Joseph F. Smith (1998), 35

Mothers and fathers have a sacred responsibility to teach and nurture their children.

joys that come from creating a home where others want to be. . . . Relief Society leaders, make sure that the meetings and the activities you plan will strengthen the homes of all your sisters."[24]

Sister Barbara W. Winder, the eleventh Relief Society general president, reminded women of spiritual blessings that come when they maintain cleanliness and order in their homes: "There is an art to being a homemaker. For ourselves and for our families, it is important that we have a sanctuary—a place of refuge away from the world where we feel comfortable and where, if others come, they, too, can feel comfortable."[25]

Individually and collectively, Relief Society sisters are examples to each other in the effort to strengthen homes and families. Sister Belle S. Spafford, the ninth Relief Society general president, shared her testimony of Relief Society's divine origin and its role in helping women fulfill their roles as wives and mothers. "I think it has a profound influence for good on the home," she said. "If one has a good mother she has a good home, and if she has a good Relief Society mother, she may be assured wisdom and a good influence will pervade the home."[26]

All sisters share the responsibility to nurture, or "mother." Elder M. Russell Ballard of the Quorum of the Twelve Apostles taught: "Sisters, we, your brethren, cannot do what you were divinely designated to do from before the foundation of the world. We may try, but we cannot ever hope to replicate your unique gifts. There is nothing in this world as personal, as nurturing, or as life changing as the influence of a righteous woman. . . . *All* women have within their divine nature both the inherent talent and the stewardship to mother."[27]

The word *motherhood* defines women's eternal roles; it describes their nature as nurturers. *Nurture* is a rich word. It means to train, to teach, to educate, to foster development, to promote growth, and to nourish or feed. Women have been given the great privilege and responsibility to nurture in all these senses of the word, and the Relief Society has the responsibility to teach and support women in their divinely ordained, indispensable roles as mothers and nurturers.[28]

Sister Julie B. Beck taught about the role of nurturing: "To nurture means to cultivate, care for, and make grow. Therefore, mothers [should] create a climate for spiritual and temporal growth in their homes. Another word for *nurturing* is *homemaking.* Homemaking includes cooking, washing clothes and dishes, and keeping an orderly home. Home is where women have the most power and influence; therefore, Latter-day Saint women should be the best homemakers in the world. Working beside children in homemaking tasks creates opportunities to teach and model qualities children should emulate. Nurturing mothers are knowledgeable, but all the education women attain will avail them nothing if they do not have the skill to make a home that creates a climate for spiritual growth. . . . Nurturing requires organization, patience, love, and work. Helping growth occur through nurturing is truly a powerful and influential role bestowed on women."[29]

Defending the Family and Motherhood

In addition to strengthening homes from the inside, the Relief Society has provided unyielding defense against influences that attack the family from the outside. President Howard W. Hunter, the fourteenth President of the Church, said:

"It seems to me that there is a great need to rally the women of the Church to stand with and for the Brethren in stemming the tide of evil that surrounds us and in moving forward the work of our Savior. . . .

". . . So we entreat you to minister with your powerful influence for good in strengthening our families, our church, and our communities."[30]

Relief Society leaders have always spoken out against efforts to weaken the traditional family and demean the sacred roles of wife and mother. Sister Amy Brown Lyman, the eighth Relief Society general president, emphasized the need for mothers to be with their children. She served as president during World War II, a time when government and civic leaders encouraged women to work outside the home to support their national economies while their husbands were at war. Some sisters needed to work outside the home to provide the necessities of life for their families. Although Sister Lyman acknowledged these challenges, she nevertheless encouraged women to do all they could to be at home and teach their children.

Sister Lyman's messages were consistent with the teachings of the First Presidency, who reminded Church members of the "sacred dedication" of motherhood.[31] President Heber J. Grant, the seventh President of the Church, and his counselors, Presidents J. Reuben Clark Jr. and David O. McKay, declared:

"Motherhood is near to divinity. It is the highest, holiest service to be assumed by mankind. It places her who honors its holy calling and service next to the angels. To you mothers in Israel we say God bless and protect you, and give you the strength and courage, the faith and knowledge, the holy love and consecration to duty, that shall enable you to fill to the fullest measure the sacred calling which is yours. To you mothers and mothers-to-be we say: Be chaste, keep pure, live righteously, that your posterity to the last generation may call you blessed."[32]

In the decades following World War II, negative influences on families and homes escalated. When President Spencer W. Kimball, the twelfth President of the Church, set apart Sister Barbara B. Smith to serve as the tenth Relief Society general president, Sister Smith felt "a profound impression of the responsibility . . . to defend the home and the woman's partnership

JULIE B. BECK
Fifteenth Relief Society General President

"The ability to qualify for, receive, and act on personal revelation is the single most important skill that can be acquired in this life. . . . It requires a conscious effort to diminish distractions, but having the spirit of revelation makes it possible to prevail over opposition and persist in faith through difficult days and essential routine tasks. . . . When we have done our very best, we may still experience disappointments, but we will not be disappointed in ourselves. We can feel certain that the Lord is pleased when we feel the Spirit working through us."

In Conference Report, Apr. 2010, 9–10; or Ensign, May 2010, 11–12

in that sacred family circle."[33] Throughout her presidency, she defended revealed truths about the divine roles of women and the blessing of eternal families. As she, her counselors, and priesthood leaders diligently studied the social issues of their day, they found that the initiatives promoted by many would not protect women's privileges in their roles as wives and mothers and would weaken families.

A newspaper reporter summarized Sister Smith's repeated message: " 'Hold your heads high, you wives, mothers, homemakers. You engender life and enrich it. Don't trade that pervasive force for fleeting, surface trinkets. Cherish it, enlarge it, magnify it. You hold a mighty office.' That's the message of the leader of Mormon women, Barbara B. Smith."[34]

Attacks on the sanctity of motherhood and the family have increased since the days of Sister Smith's presidency. But with faith in God and an understanding of the eternal significance of their responsibilities, Relief Society sisters of all ages continue to uphold and defend truths that strengthen homes and families. They guard the sanctity of the family in many different roles: as mothers and grandmothers, as daughters and sisters, as aunts, and as teachers and leaders in the Church. Whenever a woman strengthens the faith of a child, she contributes to the strength of a family—now and in the future.

Young Relief Society sisters can learn homemaking skills from more experienced sisters.

Latter-day Prophets' Teachings about the Family

A father and mother once asked their children what they had liked about a recent general conference. Their 16-year-old daughter said: "I loved it! I loved hearing inspired, intelligent prophets and leaders affirm motherhood." In her innermost feelings, this young woman had always wanted to be a mother, but she had been concerned that motherhood was unpopular and even denigrated by many people in the world. She was comforted when she heard prophets and apostles affirm the goodness of her ideals.[35] The Relief Society's work to strengthen home and family has always been unified with the teachings of latter-day prophets.

President David O. McKay, the ninth President of the Church, often taught that "no other success can compensate for failure in the home."[36]

President Harold B. Lee, the eleventh President of the Church, similarly counseled, "The most important of the Lord's work you will ever do will be within the walls of your own homes."[37]

Concerned about continuing attacks on the family, President Spencer W. Kimball prophesied and warned:

"Many of the social restraints which in the past have helped to reinforce and to shore up the family are dissolving and disappearing. The time will come when only those who believe deeply and actively in the family will be able to preserve their families in the midst of the gathering evil around us.

". . . There are those who would define the family in such a nontraditional way that they would define it out of existence. . . .

"We of all people . . . should not be taken in by the specious arguments that the family unit is somehow tied to a particular phase of development a mortal society is going through. We are free to resist those moves which downplay the significance of the family and which play up the significance of selfish individualism. We know the family to be eternal. We know that

when things go wrong in the family, things go wrong in every other institution in society."[38]

Along with these stern warnings, latter-day prophets have shared words of hope for faithful parents whose children have wandered from the gospel path. President James E. Faust said: "To those brokenhearted parents who have been righteous, diligent, and prayerful in the teaching of their disobedient children, we say to you, the Good Shepherd is watching over them. God knows and understands your deep sorrow. There is hope."[39]

President Gordon B. Hinckley expressed his confidence that Latter-day Saint women, strengthened by their association in Relief Society, can help their families withstand attacks on the home. He emphasized that Relief Society sisters can unite in defense of the family:

"It is so tremendously important that the women of the Church stand strong and immovable for that which is correct and proper under the plan of the Lord. I am convinced there is no other organization anywhere to match the Relief Society of this Church. . . . If they will be united and speak with one voice, their strength will be incalculable.

"We call upon the women of the Church to stand together for righteousness. They must begin in their own homes. They can teach it in their classes. They can voice it in their communities.

"Marriage between a man and a woman is ordained of God"
(First Presidency and Quorum of the Twelve Apostles).

"Mothers in Zion, your God-given roles are so vital to your own exaltation and to the salvation and exaltation of your family. A child needs a mother more than all the things money can buy. Spending time with your children is the greatest gift of all."

Ezra Taft Benson

The Teachings of Ezra Taft Benson *(1988)*, 515

"They must be the teachers and the guardians of their daughters. Those daughters must be taught in the Primary and in the classes of the Young Women of the values of The Church of Jesus Christ of Latter-day Saints. When you save a girl, you save generations. She will grow in strength and righteousness. She will marry in the house of the Lord. She will teach her children the ways of truth. They will walk in her paths and will similarly teach their children. Wonderful grandmothers will be there to lend encouragement."[40]

"Glimpses of Heaven"

A man once asked President Spencer W. Kimball, "Have you ever been to heaven?" In response to this question, President Kimball said that he had glimpsed heaven that very day when he had performed the sealing of a couple, one of whom was the last of 8 siblings to receive this sacred ordinance. "The pure in heart were there," President Kimball said. "Heaven was there." He told of a time when he glimpsed heaven at the home of a stake president. The home was small, but the family was large. The children worked together to set the table, and a young child offered a heartfelt prayer before supper. President Kimball said that he had glimpsed heaven when he had

Righteous women can make their homes havens where the Spirit can dwell.

spoken with a couple who had never been able to have children of their own but who had "filled their home" with 18 orphans. He shared other experiences when he had glimpsed heaven in the lives of faithful Latter-day Saints who expressed their testimonies in their words and their actions. "Heaven is a place," President Kimball taught, "but also a condition; it is home and family. It is understanding and kindness. It is interdependence and selfless activity. It is quiet, sane living; personal sacrifice, genuine hospitality, wholesome concern for others. It is living the commandments of God without ostentation or hypocrisy. It is selflessness. It is all about us. We need only to be able to recognize it as we find it and enjoy it. Yes, my dear brother, I've had many glimpses of heaven." [41]

Throughout the world, Relief Society sisters and their families have drawn near to heaven by the way they have lived.

A sister in the United States took care of her dying mother for 3 years. Less than a year later, her daughter developed a rare physical disorder. This dedicated mother took care of her daughter every day for 10 years until the young woman passed away at the age of 17.

A single mother in Tonga had a simple home where she nurtured several children. Her greatest desire was that her sons and daughters serve the Lord and improve their lives.

Righteous mothers bring up their children in the light of the gospel.

Consistent with these priorities, she helped her children establish gospel patterns in their lives. Under her leadership, they got a good education. They prayed, studied the scriptures, worked, and worshipped together.

A sister in the United States had 8 children under the age of 14. Every day was a physical, mental, spiritual, intellectual, and emotional challenge for her, but she took care of the right things. She sustained her husband in his Church service and in his efforts to support their family. Together, they prayed for each child and pondered ways to help each one advance with personal responsibilities and goals. In her home, the sheer amount of cooking, managing, thinking, and praying was tremendous for this sister. In addition, she accepted visiting teaching responsibilities and took care of sisters in her ward who needed to be lifted up. She prayed over them, worried about them, visited them, and checked on them numerous times each month.

A faithful family in Mexico lived in a busy, noisy city in a home behind a large wall and a metal gate. On the inside of the wall, the mother painted a beautiful garden, with trees, flowers, and a fountain. Inside the home, the family kept books on shelves and maintained places to gather, study, and play together.

A sister in Ghana maintained her family's farm. Outside the rail fence, she cultivated yarrow plants. Inside the fence, she kept goats in pens. She also kept palm nuts that she boiled to make palm oil to sell in the local markets. Everything in her tidy enclosure demonstrated her love for her family. She raked, cleaned, and swept her yard. Under a mango tree, the family had a homemade bench where they sat for family home evening and other family gatherings.

A single sister with physical disabilities lived on the 80th floor of a high-rise in Hong Kong. She lived alone and was the only member of the Church in her family, but she created a home that was a haven where she and visitors could feel the influence of the Spirit. On a little shelf, she kept her scriptures, her Relief Society manuals, and her hymnbook. She sought out her ancestors and traveled to the temple to perform ordinances for them.

A sister in India helped establish a branch in her city. Her husband was the branch president, and she was the Relief Society president for a group of about 20 members. They reared three faithful daughters, with the principles of the gospel safeguarding them in their holy home.

A mother in Brazil lived in a home that was made of red brick in a yard of red soil surrounded by a wall of red brick. The music of Primary songs filled the air, and pictures cut out from the *Liahona* of temples, prophets of God, and the Savior covered the walls. She and her husband sacrificed to be sealed in the temple so their children could be born in the covenant. Her constant prayer was that the Lord would help her and give her strength and inspiration sufficient to bring up her children in the light, truth, and strength of the gospel so that they would be able to make and

"To be a righteous woman during the winding up scenes on this earth . . . is an especially noble calling" (Spencer W. Kimball).

keep the covenants she and her husband had sacrificed to provide for them.

These sisters, representative of many more, are truly, as President Gordon B. Hinckley said, "guardians of the hearth." [42] They are worthy of these words spoken by President Spencer W. Kimball:

"To be a righteous woman is a glorious thing in any age. To be a righteous woman during the winding up scenes on this earth, before the second coming of our Savior, is an especially noble calling. The righteous woman's strength and influence today can be tenfold what it might be in more tranquil times. She has been placed here to help to enrich, to protect, and to guard the home—which is society's basic and most noble institution. Other institutions in society may falter and even fail, but the righteous woman can help to save the home, which may be the last and only sanctuary some mortals know in the midst of storm and strife." [43]

"May You Be Strengthened for the Challenges of the Day"

On that historic night when President Hinckley read the proclamation on the family, he concluded his address with a blessing upon the women of the Church:

"May the Lord bless you, my beloved sisters. . . . May you be strengthened for the challenges of the day. May you be endowed with wisdom beyond your own in dealing with the problems you constantly face. May your prayers and your pleadings be answered with blessings upon your heads and upon the heads of your loved ones. We leave with you our love and our blessing, that your lives may be filled with peace and gladness. It can be so. Many of you can testify that it has been so. The Lord bless you now and through the years to come, I humbly pray." [44]

The Family
A Proclamation to the World

The First Presidency and Council of the Twelve Apostles
of The Church of Jesus Christ of Latter-day Saints

We, the First Presidency and the Council of the Twelve Apostles of The Church of Jesus Christ of Latter-day Saints, solemnly proclaim that marriage between a man and a woman is ordained of God and that the family is central to the Creator's plan for the eternal destiny of His children.

All human beings—male and female—are created in the image of God. Each is a beloved spirit son or daughter of heavenly parents, and, as such, each has a divine nature and destiny. Gender is an essential characteristic of individual premortal, mortal, and eternal identity and purpose.

In the premortal realm, spirit sons and daughters knew and worshipped God as their Eternal Father and accepted His plan by which His children could obtain a physical body and gain earthly experience to progress toward perfection and ultimately realize their divine destiny as heirs of eternal life. The divine plan of happiness enables family relationships to be perpetuated beyond the grave. Sacred ordinances and covenants available in holy temples make it possible for individuals to return to the presence of God and for families to be united eternally.

The first commandment that God gave to Adam and Eve pertained to their potential for parenthood as husband and wife. We declare that God's commandment for His children to multiply and replenish the earth remains in force. We further declare that God has commanded that the sacred powers of procreation are to be employed only between man and woman, lawfully wedded as husband and wife.

We declare the means by which mortal life is created to be divinely appointed. We affirm the sanctity of life and of its importance in God's eternal plan.

Husband and wife have a solemn responsibility to love and care for each other and for their children. "Children are an heritage of the Lord" (Psalm 127:3). Parents have a sacred duty to rear their children in love and righteousness, to provide for their physical and spiritual needs, and to teach them to love and serve one another, observe the commandments of God, and be law-abiding citizens wherever they live. Husbands and wives—mothers and fathers—will be held accountable before God for the discharge of these obligations.

The family is ordained of God. Marriage between man and woman is essential to His eternal plan. Children are entitled to birth within the bonds of matrimony, and to be reared by a father and a mother who honor marital vows with complete fidelity. Happiness in family life is most likely to be achieved when founded upon the teachings of the Lord Jesus Christ. Successful marriages and families are established and maintained on principles of faith, prayer, repentance, forgiveness, respect, love, compassion, work, and wholesome recreational activities. By divine design, fathers are to preside over their families in love and righteousness and are responsible to provide the necessities of life and protection for their families. Mothers are primarily responsible for the nurture of their children. In these sacred responsibilities, fathers and mothers are obligated to help one another as equal partners. Disability, death, or other circumstances may necessitate individual adaptation. Extended families should lend support when needed.

We warn that individuals who violate covenants of chastity, who abuse spouse or offspring, or who fail to fulfill family responsibilities will one day stand accountable before God. Further, we warn that the disintegration of the family will bring upon individuals, communities, and nations the calamities foretold by ancient and modern prophets.

We call upon responsible citizens and officers of government everywhere to promote those measures designed to maintain and strengthen the family as the fundamental unit of society.

This proclamation was read by President Gordon B. Hinckley as part of his message at the General Relief Society Meeting held September 23, 1995, in Salt Lake City, Utah.

"Live Up to Your Privilege"

You are now placed in a situation where you can act according to those sympathies which God has planted in your bosoms. If you live up to these principles how great and glorious!—if you live up to your privilege, the angels cannot be restrained from being your associates. . . . If you will be pure, nothing can hinder.

Joseph Smith

"Live Up to Your Privilege"

In one of the first meetings of the Female Relief Society of Nauvoo, Joseph Smith admonished the sisters to "live up to [their] privilege."[1] With that encouragement as a foundation, sisters in The Church of Jesus Christ of Latter-day Saints have been taught to live up to their divine potential by fulfilling God's purposes for them. As they come to understand who they really are—God's daughters, with an innate capacity to love

and nurture—they reach their potential as holy women. With charity in their hearts, they fulfill the purposes of Relief Society: to increase faith and personal righteousness, strengthen families and homes, and seek out and help those in need.

Established as an integral part of the Restoration, the Relief Society helps Latter-day Saint women live up to their privilege. Through this organization, sisters receive a vision and assurance of their identity as daughters of God. They also receive opportunities to serve and the direction and authority they need to fulfill those responsibilities.

God has blessed His daughters with great capacity to love and nurture.

Daughters of God

Joseph Smith taught Relief Society sisters of their nobility as daughters of God, helping them understand that God loved them and had grand purposes for them to fulfill. Women in the Church play essential roles in Heavenly Father's plan of salvation—just as important as the roles played by men who hold the priesthood. The Lord has endowed women with an innate desire to serve and bless others, and He has entrusted them with a sacred responsibility to use their gifts to help save His children.

Women sometimes forget their true nobility and give in to the diversions and temptations of the world. Concerned about this trend, Sister Mary Ellen Smoot, the thirteenth Relief Society general president, and her counselors, Sisters Virginia U. Jensen and Sheri L. Dew, felt a need to help the women of the Church remember their identity. In a general Relief Society meeting, they expressed what it means to be daughters of God:

"We are beloved spirit daughters of God, and our lives have meaning, purpose, and direction. As a worldwide sisterhood, we are united in our devotion to Jesus Christ, our Savior and Exemplar. We are women of faith, virtue, vision, and charity who:

"Increase our testimonies of Jesus Christ through prayer and scripture study.

"Seek spiritual strength by following the promptings of the Holy Ghost.

"Dedicate ourselves to strengthening marriages, families, and homes.

"Find nobility in motherhood and joy in womanhood.

"Delight in service and good works.

"Love life and learning.

"Stand for truth and righteousness.

"Sustain the priesthood as the authority of God on earth.

"Rejoice in the blessings of the temple, understand our divine destiny, and strive for exaltation."[2]

Priesthood leaders have also reminded women of their divine nature and sacred responsibilities. Elder M. Russell Ballard of the Quorum of the Twelve Apostles said: "We believe in and are counting on your goodness and your strength, your propensity for virtue and valor, your kindness and courage, your strength and resilience. We believe in your mission as women of God. . . . We believe that the Church simply will not accomplish what it must without your faith and faithfulness, your innate tendency to put the well-being of others ahead of your own, and your spiritual strength and tenacity. And we believe that God's plan is for you to become queens and to receive the highest blessings any woman can receive in time or eternity."[3]

As women live up to their privilege and potential as daughters of God, they prepare themselves for the blessing of eternal life. This is the glorious destiny God has in store for His faithful daughters.

True Charity, a Legacy Passed from Heart to Heart

The Prophet Joseph Smith taught, "It is natural for females to have feelings of charity."

As women live up to their potential as daughters of God, they prepare themselves for the blessings of eternal life.

With the establishment of Relief Society, he told the sisters, "You are now placed in a situation where you can act according to those sympathies which God has planted in your bosoms."[4] For true charity to blossom in their hearts, women must combine their innate compassion with faith in Jesus Christ and His Atonement. President Henry B. Eyring, a counselor in the First Presidency, explained that this true charity is the legacy of Relief Society:

"I will speak to you . . . of the great legacy those who went before you in the Relief Society have passed on to you. The part . . . which seems to me most important and persistent is that charity is at the heart of the society and is to come into the heart, to be part of the very nature, of every member. Charity meant to them far more than a feeling of benevolence. Charity is born of faith in the Lord Jesus Christ and is an effect of His Atonement working in the hearts of the members. . . .

"This society is composed of women whose feelings of charity spring from hearts changed by qualifying for and by keeping covenants offered only in the Lord's true Church. Their feelings of charity come from Him through His Atonement.

Henry B. Eyring

Their acts of charity are guided by His example—and come out of gratitude for His infinite gift of mercy—and by the Holy Spirit, which He sends to accompany His servants on their missions of mercy."[5]

This legacy of charity began with the sisters in Nauvoo, who engaged in organized charitable works and received temple covenants. It continued in Winter Quarters and along the arduous trail to the Salt Lake Valley. It sustained Latter-day Saint women as they settled frontier communities, endured political persecution and world wars, and maintained hope during economic depression. It has inspired loving-kindness at home and outreach efforts

worldwide. It has motivated Relief Society sisters as they have served in hospitals and as they have helped with adoptions, wheat storage, humanitarian aid, and welfare. The pure love of Christ continues to motivate Relief Society sisters today as they gather to teach and serve one another and as they strengthen and watch over each other one by one.

Every Latter-day Saint woman becomes a part of this legacy of love and has the responsibility and privilege to share this heritage with others.

One family's history illustrates how the Relief Society heritage has been passed from mother to daughter for generations. Each daughter has embraced the Relief Society's motto, "Charity never faileth."

The legacy began with Elizabeth Haven Barlow, who joined the Church in 1837. Elizabeth became a member of the Female Relief Society of Nauvoo on April 28, 1842, and she heard the Prophet Joseph Smith teach the foundational principles of the organization. These teachings sustained her through a life that included being a victim of mobbings and persecution, bearing a child during the journey to the Salt Lake Valley, and caring for a young family while her husband was on a mission. She served as a Relief Society president in Bountiful, Utah, from 1857 to 1888, three years prior to her death at age 81.

The story continued with her daughter Pamela Barlow Thompson. Pamela and her husband were called to settle Panaca, Nevada, where she became a Relief Society president. She taught the sisters homemaking skills, including how to use a new mechanical marvel: the sewing machine. When they were living in Nevada, her husband was killed. She and her large family then moved to Bountiful, Utah, where she was again called to serve in a Relief Society presidency.

Pamela passed this legacy to her daughter Theresa Thompson Call. Soon after Theresa was married, she and her husband moved to Mexico. During most of her life, she served simultaneously as the Relief Society president and a counselor in the Primary presidency. She was well known for her compassionate service, taking meals to the needy. She made a practice of taking cakes to her elderly neighbors on their birthdays. On one such occasion, she forgot a neighbor's birthday until after supper. Committed to the principle that "charity never faileth," she rekindled the fire in the stove and stirred up a cake. When she arrived at the door late that night, the sister burst into tears and

"The history of Relief Society is recorded in words and numbers, but the heritage is passed heart to heart" (Henry B. Eyring).

said, "I have been waiting all day for you, and I had just about decided that you had forgotten me this time."

Theresa's daughter Athelia Call Sears also loved Relief Society. She rushed to get her ironing done every Tuesday morning so she could attend Relief Society meeting on Tuesday afternoon. In her 70s, she was called to serve as a ward Relief Society president. At a time when wards were required to raise funds for equipment and activities, she led her Relief Society sisters in raising enough money to buy kitchen equipment for the meetinghouse, with an additional $1,000 for the bishop to use for other needs in the ward.

The pure love of Christ continues to inspire Relief Society sisters as they teach and serve one another.

Athelia Sears Tanner, a daughter of Sister Sears, was called as a young mother to be a ward Relief Society president. Much of her compassionate service consisted of tending for and taking meals to mothers of new babies. A natural teacher with a strong testimony of Jesus Christ, she nurtured her 13 children and also served others and saved souls in various capacities in Relief Society throughout her life.

The legacy of charity has continued in this family. All of Sister Tanner's daughters have served faithfully in Relief Society, and her granddaughters have followed their mothers' examples.[6]

Charitable service is the spiritual legacy of every member of Relief Society. As President Eyring explained: "You pass the heritage along as you help others receive the gift of charity in their hearts. They will then be able to pass it to others. The history of Relief Society is recorded in words and numbers, but the heritage is passed heart to heart."[7]

"My Turn to Serve"

After recounting many examples of people with great faith, the Apostle Paul said, "Seeing we also are compassed about with so great a cloud of witnesses, let us lay aside every weight, and the sin which doth so easily beset us, and let us run with patience the race that is set before us, looking unto Jesus the author and finisher of our faith."[8]

The women of the Church are surrounded by a great host of witnesses, including "our glorious Mother Eve" and "many of her faithful daughters who [have] lived through the ages and worshiped the true and living God."[9] Faithful daughters of God live up to their privilege by following in the footsteps of these witnesses, laying aside the problems and temptations that beset them and running the race that the Lord sets before them.

Every generation has noble, charitable, faithful, holy women. Although few of these women will have their names recorded in history, their Heavenly Father knows them well. And this, as Eliza R. Snow said, is all that ultimately matters: "There are many of the sisters whose labors are not known beyond their own dwellings and perhaps not appreciated there, but what difference does that make? If your labors are acceptable to God, however simple the duties, if faithfully performed, you should never be discouraged."[10]

The following story is one of the countless examples of the influence of faithful Relief Society sisters. In this case, a handful of women touched the life of a young adult named Lynne. Because Lynne saw these sisters serve, she was determined to do the same when she became a Relief Society sister.

Mothers can share the heritage of Relief Society with their daughters.

When Lynne was in her late teens, she and her mother learned that her stepfather had been seriously injured in a distant city. They quickly got on an airplane to visit him, but he died before they could reach him. Lynne later told about what happened upon their return home:

"As my mother and I, exhausted and heartsick, walked down the steps from the plane, [a] man and woman standing on the airstrip walked over and put their arms around us. It was the branch president and the Relief Society president. . . .

"Those days were confusing as we struggled to deal with the fact that [my stepfather] was dead. . . . But there was always a sister there, waiting quietly in the background—to take messages, to answer the door, to hold our hands as we made phone calls to our families and friends. They were there to help us pack, to deal with all that had to be done.

"Through it all, I developed such a sense of gratitude that I couldn't imagine how I could repay those dear sisters. I desperately tried to think of a way, but imagination gave way to exhaustion."

Several years later, when Lynne was married with three small children, she was called to serve in a Relief Society presidency. At times she wondered if she could meet the demands of her calling. But then she remembered the service she had received after her stepfather died. "Now," she thought to herself, "it's my turn." She shared the following experiences:

"A woman in the ward had lost her fourteen-year-old daughter. The mother asked me to buy a beautiful gown and to dress her daughter's body in it in preparation for the burial. I was able to do it—and found it a very tender experience. It was my turn to serve, as [other sisters] had served me.

"An elderly woman in the ward who lived alone overdosed on her medications and was in a helpless condition for three days. The other counselor and I found her still alive in her apartment and cleaned her up before the ambulance arrived. We then stayed to scrub the apartment—walls and floors—with disinfectant. My turn again.

"A young mother in the ward, one of my friends, suddenly lost her only child, a beautiful three-year-old daughter, to an infection that took her life before the doctors were even aware of how serious her illness was. The other counselor and I went to the house as soon as we heard of little Robin's death. As we approached the screened patio door, we heard the father (who was not a member of the Church) sobbing as he talked long distance to his mother. Looking up, he saw us and, still sobbing, spoke into the phone: 'It will be all right, Mother. The Mormon women are here.' My turn once more."

Lynne later commented that when people asked her what she thought of Relief Society, she told them about her experiences receiving and giving service. She said: "That's how I feel about Relief Society way down deep. And why."[11]

All over the world, Latter-day Saint women feel the same way about Relief Society, "way down deep." Like Lynne, they have benefited from Relief Society service, and they know it is now their turn to serve with charity and faith. They give this service in different capacities—as daughters, wives, mothers, sisters, aunts, visiting teachers, Relief Society leaders, neighbors, and friends. Some of their service comes in response to assignments from Church leaders, and some of their service comes in response to quiet promptings from the Holy Ghost. Seeing that they are "compassed about with so great a cloud of witnesses," they are ready to "run with patience the race that is set before [them]."

"Lead the World . . . in Everything That Is Praise-Worthy"

President Joseph F. Smith, the sixth President of the Church, urged Latter-day Saint women to "lead the world and to lead especially the women of the world, in everything that is praise-worthy, everything that is

"For such a time as this" (Esther 4:14)

"I believe when we determine within our hearts that by and with the blessings of God our Heavenly Father we will accomplish a certain labor, God gives the ability to accomplish that labor; but when we lay down, when we become discouraged, when we look at the top of the mountain and say it is impossible to climb to the summit, while we never make an effort it will never be accomplished."

Heber J. Grant

Teachings of Presidents of the Church: Heber J. Grant (2002), 37

God-like, everything that is uplifting and that is purifying." He said, "You are called by the voice of the Prophet of God to do it, to be uppermost, to be the greatest and the best, the purest and the most devoted to the right."[12]

Throughout the history of the Lord's restored Church, female disciples of Christ have lived up to this standard. Like Esther, they have been faithful and courageous in the face of difficult challenges. They have found purpose in their lives, as Esther did when her cousin Mordecai asked her, "Who knoweth whether thou art come to the kingdom for such a time as this?"[13] Like Nehemiah in the Old Testament, they have not been diverted from their sacred responsibilities. When Nehemiah's enemies tried to tempt him away from his duty to rebuild the wall of Jerusalem, he replied, "I am doing a great work, so that I cannot come down: why should the work cease, whilst I leave it, and come down to you?"[14] His enemies continued to tempt him, but he stayed strong and true

In each new generation, Relief Society sisters can say, "Now it is our turn to serve."

to his important work. The world has tried to persuade the women of the Church to abandon their God-given missions, but faithful Relief Society sisters have not "come down."

The charge to lead out in everything that is praiseworthy, Godlike, uplifting, and purifying is a demanding one. It always has been. But individual Relief Society sisters are not alone in accepting this charge. They are part of a great organization, founded by priesthood authority and strengthened by the teachings and declarations of prophets. They are beloved daughters of God with sacred responsibilities. They are covenant people of the Lamb, "armed with righteousness and with the power of God in great glory."[15] As they unite with other faithful Saints and learn from the examples of those who have gone before, they can prevail over mortal challenges. They can help build the kingdom of God throughout the world and in their homes. They can say, "Now it is our turn—our turn to serve and write a chapter on the pages of Relief Society's history." With an assurance of Heavenly Father's love for them and a testimony of the power of the Atonement of Jesus Christ, they can rise above ordinary thoughts and ambitions and be part of "something extraordinary."[16]

The Lord's promises are sure as sisters follow the counsel He gave to the first Relief Society president: "Verily I say unto you, all those who receive my gospel are sons and daughters in my kingdom. . . . Lay aside the things of this world, and seek for the things of a better. . . . Cleave unto the covenants which thou hast made."[17] When the Prophet Joseph Smith told Relief Society sisters to "live up to [their] privilege," he combined that exhortation with a promise: "The angels cannot be restrained from being your associates. . . . If you will be pure, nothing can hinder."[18]

History of Relief Society

APRIL 6, 1830
The Church is organized.

1830
Joseph Smith receives a revelation for his wife Emma (see D&C 25).

MARCH 17, 1842
The Female Relief Society of Nauvoo is organized; Emma Smith is chosen as president.

1843
Emma Smith and her counselors appoint visiting committees in the wards in Nauvoo, Illinois.

JUNE 27, 1844
The Prophet Joseph Smith and his brother Hyrum are martyred at the Carthage Jail.

FEBRUARY 1846
The Saints begin leaving Nauvoo.

1846
The Nauvoo Temple is dedicated.

JULY 1847
The first pioneer company reaches the Salt Lake Valley.

1867
Brigham Young calls on bishops to reestablish the Relief Society in every ward.

1870
The Young Ladies Department of the Cooperative Junior and Senior Retrenchment Association is established for young women.

1872
The Relief Society supports the publishing of the *Woman's Exponent.*

1873
Relief Society sisters are encouraged to receive medical training.

1876
The Deseret Silk Association is established, with Zina D. H. Young as president.

1878
The Primary organization is established for children.

1882
The Relief Society establishes the Deseret Hospital.

1890
Wilford Woodruff receives a revelation leading to the discontinuance of the practice of plural marriage.

1893
The Salt Lake Temple is dedicated.

1913
"Charity never faileth" becomes the Relief Society motto.

1915
The Relief Society begins publishing the *Relief Society Magazine.*

1916
Visiting teachers begin discussing a gospel message with sisters each month.

1918
The Relief Society sells 200,000 bushels of wheat to the United States government.

1921
The Relief Society establishes a maternity hospital.

1936
The First Presidency establishes the Church welfare program.

1944
Visiting teachers stop collecting donations and focus instead on ministering to the sisters they visit.

1954
Belle S. Spafford leads the United States delegation at the International Council of Women.

1956
The Relief Society Building is dedicated in Salt Lake City.

1969

The Relief Society Social Service Department is incorporated into Church Welfare and Social Services.

1971

The *Relief Society Magazine* is discontinued and replaced with the *Ensign*.

1978

The Monument to Women Memorial Garden is dedicated in Nauvoo.

SEPTEMBER 16, 1978

The first general Relief Society meeting is held.

1987

A monthly visiting teaching message is included in the international magazine (now the *Liahona*) and the *Ensign*.

1992

Sisters celebrate the 150th anniversary of the Relief Society by participating in service projects in their communities.

SEPTEMBER 23, 1995

President Gordon B. Hinckley reads "The Family: A Proclamation to the World" in a general Relief Society meeting.

1997

Relief Societies, high priests groups, and elders quorums begin to study from the same curriculum on Sundays.

2004

Relief Society, Young Women, and Primary general presidents participate in the first worldwide leadership training meeting for auxiliaries.

2009

Relief Society membership reaches 6 million.

Sisters at general Relief Society meeting

2011

The Church observes the 75th anniversary of the welfare program.

WELFARE SQUARE

THE CHURCH OF JESUS CHRIST OF LATTER DAY SAINTS

Relief Society
General Presidencies

President: Emma Hale Smith, 1842–44.
First Counselor: Sarah Marietta Kingsley Cleveland, 1842–44. **Second Counselor:** Elizabeth Ann Smith Whitney, 1842–44.

President: Eliza Roxcy Snow, 1866–87.
First Counselor: Zina Diantha Huntington Young, 1880–88. **Second Counselor:** Elizabeth Ann Smith Whitney, 1880–82.

President: Zina Diantha Huntington Young, 1888–1901. **First Counselor:** Jane Snyder Richards, 1888–1901. **Second Counselor:** Bathsheba Wilson Smith, 1888–1901.

President: Bathsheba Wilson Smith, 1901–10.
First Counselor: Annie Taylor Hyde, 1901–9.
Second Counselor: Ida Smoot Dusenberry, 1901–10.

President: Emmeline Woodward B. Wells, 1910–21. **First Counselor:** Clarissa Smith Williams, 1910–21. **Second Counselor:** Julina Lambson Smith, 1910–21.

President: Clarissa Smith Williams, 1921–28.
First Counselor: Jennie Brimhall Knight, 1921–28.
Second Counselor: Louise Yates Robison, 1921–28.

President: Louise Yates Robison, 1928–39.
First Counselor: Amy Brown Lyman, 1928–39.
Second Counselors: Julia Alleman Child, 1928–35; Kate Montgomery Barker, 1935–39.

President: Amy Brown Lyman, 1940–45.
First Counselor: Marcia Knowlton Howells, 1940–45. **Second Counselors:** Donna Durrant Sorensen, 1940–42; Belle Smith Spafford, 1942–45.

President: Belle Smith Spafford, 1945–74.
First Counselor: Marianne Clark Sharp, 1945–74. **Second Counselors:** Gertrude Ryberg Garff, 1945–47; Velma Nebeker Simonsen, 1947–56; Helen Woodruff Anderson, 1957–58; Louise Wallace Madsen, 1958–74.

President: Barbara Bradshaw Smith, 1974–84.
First Counselors: Janath Russell Cannon, 1974–78; Marian Richards Boyer, 1978–84.
Second Counselors: Marian Richards Boyer, 1974–78; Shirley Wilkes Thomas, 1978–83; Ann Stoddard Reese, 1983–84.

President: Barbara Woodhead Winder, 1984–90.
First Counselor: Joy Frewin Evans, 1984–90.
Second Counselor: Joanne Bushman Doxey, 1984–90.

President: Elaine Low Jack, 1990–97.
First Counselor: Chieko Nishimura Okazaki, 1990–97. **Second Counselor:** Aileen Hales Clyde, 1990–97.

President: Mary Ellen Wood Smoot, 1997–2002.
First Counselor: Virginia Urry Jensen, 1997–2002.
Second Counselor: Sheri L. Dew, 1997–2002.

President: Bonnie Dansie Parkin, 2002–7.
First Counselor: Kathleen Hurst Hughes, 2002–7.
Second Counselor: Anne Clark Pingree, 2002–7.

President: Julie Bangerter Beck, beginning in 2007. **First Counselor:** Silvia Henriquez Allred, beginning in 2007. **Second Counselor:** Barbara Thompson, beginning in 2007.

Notes

Preface

1. Emma Smith, in Relief Society Minute Book, Nauvoo, Illinois, Mar. 17, 1842, Church History Library, 12.

2. Spencer W. Kimball, "Privileges and Responsibilities of Sisters," *Ensign*, Nov. 1978, 104.

3. Belle S. Spafford, *A Woman's Reach* (1974), 23.

4. Alma 37:6.

Chapter 1

1. James E. Talmage, *Jesus the Christ*, 3rd ed. (1916), 475.

2. See John 19:25–27.

3. See John 20:1–18.

4. See Luke 10:38–42.

5. See John 11:20–27.

6. Luke 8:1–3.

7. 1 Timothy 5:10.

8. Titus 2:4.

9. Acts 9:36–40.

10. See Romans 16:3–5.

11. 1 Corinthians 16:19; italics added.

12. Romans 16:6.

13. See Acts 16:14–15.

14. Romans 16:1–2; italics added.

15. Joseph Smith, quoted in Sarah M. Kimball, "Auto-biography," *Woman's Exponent*, Sept. 1, 1883, 51; see also *Teachings of Presidents of the Church: Joseph Smith* (2007), 451.

16. Eliza R. Snow, "Female Relief Society," *Deseret News*, Apr. 22, 1868, 1; punctuation standardized.

17. *Teachings of Presidents of the Church: Joseph F. Smith* (1998), 184.

18. Lorenzo Snow, in "Prest. Snow to Relief Societies," *Deseret Evening News*, July 9, 1901, 1.

19. Julie B. Beck, "What Latter-day Saint Women Do Best: Stand Strong and Immovable," *Ensign*, Nov. 2007, 109.

Chapter 2

1. Sarah M. Kimball, in Record of the Relief Society from First Organization to Conference, Apr. 5, 1892, Book II, Church History Library, 29; spelling and capitalization standardized.

2. Sarah M. Kimball, "Auto-biography," *Woman's Exponent*, Sept. 1, 1883, 51.

3. See Relief Society Minute Book, Nauvoo, Illinois, Mar. 17, 1842, 6–7; twenty sisters attended the first meeting, and seven who were not in attendance were accepted into the society as part of that meeting.

4. Joseph Smith, in Relief Society Minute Book, Nauvoo, Illinois, Mar. 17, 1842, Church History Library, 7; spelling, punctuation, and capitalization standardized as needed in all excerpts from this minute book.

5. See Relief Society Minute Book, Nauvoo, Illinois, Mar. 17, 1842, 8–9.

6. Doctrine and Covenants 25:3, 7.

7. See Joseph Smith, in Relief Society Minute Book, Nauvoo, Illinois, Mar. 17, 1842, 8.

8. See Doctrine and Covenants 25:2, 5–8, 10–11, 13–15.

9. Doctrine and Covenants 25:16.

10. Joseph Smith, in Relief Society Minute Book, Nauvoo, Illinois, Mar. 17, 1842, 8.

11. Emma Smith, in Relief Society Minute Book, Nauvoo, Illinois, Mar. 17, 1842, 12.

12. See Relief Society Minute Book, Nauvoo, Illinois, Mar. 17, 1842, 14.

13. Joseph Smith, in Relief Society Minute Book, Nauvoo, Illinois, Apr. 28, 1842, 40.

14. Joseph Smith, in Relief Society Minute Book, Nauvoo, Illinois, Mar. 30, 1842, 22.

15. Joseph Smith, in Relief Society Minute Book, Nauvoo, Illinois, Apr. 28, 1842, 38.

16. Boyd K. Packer, in Conference Report, Oct. 1978, 9–10; or *Ensign*, Nov. 1978, 8.

17. See Joseph Smith, in Relief Society Minute Book, Nauvoo, Illinois, Mar. 17, 1842, 8.

18. Eliza R. Snow, in Relief Society Minute Book, Nauvoo, Illinois, Apr. 28, 1842, 41.

19. See Joseph Smith, in Relief Society Minute Book, Nauvoo, Illinois, June 9, 1842, 63.

20. Joseph Smith, in Relief Society Minute Book, Nauvoo, Illinois, June 9, 1842, 63.

21. Joseph Smith, in Relief Society Minute Book, Nauvoo, Illinois, June 9, 1842, 63.

22. Joseph Smith, in Relief Society Minute Book, Nauvoo, Illinois, Apr. 28, 1842, 38.

23. Joseph Smith, in Relief Society Minute Book, Nauvoo, Illinois, Apr. 28, 1842, 35.

24. Doctrine and Covenants 20:69.

25. Joseph Smith, in Relief Society Minute Book, Nauvoo, Illinois, Apr. 28, 1842, 38.

26. Doctrine and Covenants 25:5.

27. Doctrine and Covenants 68:25–28.

28. Doctrine and Covenants 93:40, 44, 49–50.

29. Emma Smith, in Relief Society Minute Book, Nauvoo, Illinois, Mar. 9, 1844, 123.

30. Joseph Smith, in Relief Society Minute Book, Nauvoo, Illinois, Apr. 28, 1842, 40.

31. *Teachings of Presidents of the Church: Joseph Smith* (2007), 482.

32. In Relief Society Minute Book, Nauvoo, Illinois, Apr. 14, 1842, 28.

33. In Relief Society Minute Book, Nauvoo, Illinois, Aug. 5, 1843, 103.

34. In Relief Society Minute Book, Nauvoo, Illinois, Aug. 13, 1843, 107.

35. In Relief Society Minute Book, Nauvoo, Illinois, Meeting of the Female Relief Society of the Third Ward, no date, 112.

36. Doctrine and Covenants 124:27–30.

37. See Doctrine and Covenants 131–32.

38. Sally Randall, in Kenneth W. Godfrey, *Women's Voices: An Untold History of the Latter-day Saints* (1982), 138–39.

39. Matthew 25:40.

40. "R. S. Reports," *Woman's Exponent,* Sept. 1, 1876, 50.

41. Joseph Smith, quoted in Edward W. Tullidge, *The Women of Mormondom* (1877), 76.

42. In Relief Society Minute Book, Nauvoo, Illinois, June 16, 1843, 91–92.

43. Joseph Smith, in Relief Society Minute Book, Nauvoo, Illinois, Apr. 28, 1842, 39.

44. Joseph Smith, in Relief Society Minute Book, Nauvoo, Illinois, June 9, 1842, 62.

45. Ellen Douglas, letter, dated Apr. 14, 1844, typescript, Church History Library.

46. John A. Widtsoe, *Evidences and Reconciliations,* arr. G. Homer Durham, 3 vols. in 1 (1960), 308.

47. Emily Woodmansee, "As Sisters in Zion," *Hymns,* no. 309.

48. M. Russell Ballard, "Women of Righteousness," *Ensign,* Apr. 2002, 70.

49. Lucy Mack Smith, in Relief Society Minute Book, Nauvoo, Illinois, Mar. 24, 1842, 18–19.

Chapter 3

1. Doctrine and Covenants 25:13.

2. Alma 27:27.

3. Brigham Young, in *History of the Church,* 7:567.

4. Sarah DeArmon Pea Rich, "Autobiography, 1885–93," Church History Library, 66; spelling, punctuation, and capitalization standardized; quoted by Richard G. Scott, in Conference Report, Apr. 2009, 42; or *Ensign,* May 2009, 44–45.

5. Doctrine and Covenants 136:4.

6. In Charles Lanman, *A Summer in the Wilderness* (1847), 32.

7. Doctrine and Covenants 136:1, 8.

8. Presendia Lathrop Kimball, "A Venerable Woman," *Woman's Exponent,* June 1, 1883, 9.

9. Drusilla Dorris Hendricks, "Historical Sketch of James Hendricks and Drusilla Dorris Hendricks," in *Henry Hendricks Genealogy,* comp. Marguerite Allen (1963), 28.

10. See Jill Mulvay Derr, Janath Russell Cannon, and Maureen Ursenbach Beecher, *Women of Covenant: The Story of Relief Society* (1992), 67.

11. Journal of Eliza Partridge Lyman, July 14–Dec. 12, 1846, Church History Library, 32–35.

12. Journal of Eliza Partridge Lyman, 38.

13. Autobiography of Bathsheba W. Smith, typescript, Church History Library, 13; punctuation, spelling, and capitalization standardized.

14. Helen Mar Whitney, "Scenes and Incidents at Winter Quarters," *Woman's Exponent,* Dec. 1, 1885, 98.

15. Wallace Stegner, *The Gathering of Zion: The Story of the Mormon Trail* (1981), 13.

16. Alma 34:28.

17. Emmeline B. Wells, "After the Days of Nauvoo," in Record of the Relief Society from First Organization to Conference, Apr. 5, 1892, Book II, Church History Library, 234–35; spelling and capitalization standardized.

18. Brigham Young, "Remarks," *Deseret News,* Oct. 15, 1856, 252.

19. Lucy Meserve Smith, "Historical Sketches of My Great Grandfathers," manuscript, Special Collections, Marriott Library, University of Utah, 53–54; spelling, capitalization, and punctuation standardized.

20. Moroni 7:47.

21. Lucy Meserve Smith, "Historical Sketches of My Great Grandfathers," 54.

Chapter 4

1. See Journal of Wilford Woodruff, Dec. 26, 1866, Church History Library.

2. Brigham Young, "Remarks," *Deseret Evening News,* Dec. 14, 1867, 2; see also *Teachings of Presidents of the Church: Brigham Young* (1997), 131.

3. Joseph Smith, in Relief Society Minute Book, Nauvoo, Illinois, Apr. 28, 1842, Church History Library, 38; spelling standardized.

4. Eliza R. Snow, "Female Relief Society," *Deseret News,* Apr. 22, 1868, 81.

5. Eliza R. Snow, "Female Relief Society," 81.

6. Eliza R. Snow, in Relief Society Minutes, Third Ward, Salt Lake Stake, Sept. 23, 1868, Church History Library, 17.

7. Brigham Young, quoted in *The Personal Writings of Eliza Roxcy Snow,* ed. Maureen Ursenbach Beecher (1995), 35.

8. Doctrine and Covenants 25:7.

9. Eliza R. Snow, "Female Relief Society," 81.

10. Brigham Young, "Remarks," *Deseret News Weekly,* May 13, 1868, 3; punctuation standardized.

11. In Susa Young Gates, *History of the Young Ladies' Mutual Improvement Association* (1911), 9–10.

12. Eliza R. Snow, in Senior and Junior Cooperative Retrenchment Association Minutes, Feb. 20, 1875, typescript, Church History Library; punctuation standardized.

13. Letter from Eliza R. Snow to Mary Elizabeth Lightner, May 27, 1869, Church History Library.

14. Eliza R. Snow, "An Address by Miss Eliza R. Snow," *Millennial Star,* Jan. 13, 1874, 18.

15. See Doctrine and Covenants 132.

16. Eliza R. Snow, in Relief Society Minutes, Fifteenth Ward, Salt Lake Stake, Jan. 6, 1870, Church History Library, 140; punctuation and capitalization standardized.

17. In "Great Indignation Meeting," *Millennial Star,* Feb. 22, 1870, 115.

18. "The Mormon Question," *New York Times,* Feb. 8, 1870, 1.

19. "Mormon Women in Council," *New York Herald,* Jan. 23, 1870; quoted in *Deseret News,* Feb. 16, 1870, 23.

20. Wilford Woodruff, "Remarks," *Deseret Weekly,* Nov. 14, 1891, 660.

21. Diary of Zina D. H. Young, Oct. 6, 1890, Church History Library; spelling standardized.

22. Helen Mar Whitney, *A Woman's View: Helen Mar Whitney's Reminiscences of Early Church History,* ed. Richard N. Holzapfel and Jeni B. Holzapfel (1997), 140.

23. See Andrew Jenson, *Latter-day Saint Biographical Encyclopedia,* 4 vols. (1901–36), 1:695.

24. Eliza R. Snow, in Tenth Ward Relief Society Minutes, Jan. 22, 1874, Church History Library, 24; punctuation and capitalization standardized.

25. Emily S. Richards, in "General Conference Relief Society," *Woman's Exponent,* Dec. 1901, 54.

26. In "Emily S. Richards," *Brigham Young University Bulletin: Dedicatory Services for Naming and Dedication of Twelve Buildings,* May 7, 1957, 21.

27. Spencer W. Kimball, "The Role of Righteous Women," *Ensign,* Nov. 1979, 102, 104.

28. See *Teachings of Presidents of the Church: Brigham Young,* 167–68.

29. Brigham Young, "Remarks," *Deseret News Weekly,* May 13, 1868, 3.

30. Eliza R. Snow, "Female Relief Society," 81.

31. Brigham Young, "Remarks," *Deseret News Weekly,* May 13, 1868, 3.

32. Emmeline B. Wells, "Be Wise and Hearken to Counsel," *Woman's Exponent,* Nov. 1, 1876, 84; punctuation standardized.

33. Sarah Howard, in "General Meeting of Central and Ward Committees," *Woman's Exponent,* Dec. 1, 1876, 99.

34. John Taylor, "Discourse by Prest. John Taylor," *Deseret News,* Apr. 9, 1879, 147.

35. Emmeline B. Wells, "Sisters Be in Earnest," *Woman's Exponent,* Oct. 15, 1876, 76.

36. See Jill Mulvay Derr, Janath Russell Cannon, and Maureen Ursenbach Beecher, *Women of Covenant: The Story of Relief Society* (1992), 165–66.

37. See "Church Wheat to Be Turned Over to Government," *Deseret Evening News,* May 20, 1918, 1.

38. Eliza R. Snow, "An Address," *Woman's Exponent,* Sept. 15, 1873, 63.

39. Emmeline B. Wells, "Zina D. H. Young—A Character Sketch," *Improvement Era,* Nov. 1901, 45.

40. Eliza R. Snow, "An Address by Miss Eliza R. Snow," 20; punctuation standardized.

41. Emma Andersen Liljenquist, in *Our Pioneer Heritage,* comp. Kate B. Carter (1963), 6:445–46.

42. "Deseret Hospital," *Woman's Exponent,* Aug. 1, 1882, 36.

43. Diary of Emmeline B. Wells, Jan. 4, 1878, Harold B. Lee Library Special Collections, Brigham Young University; punctuation standardized.

44. Diary of Emmeline B. Wells, Aug. 1, 1895.

45. Eliza R. Snow, "An Address by Miss Eliza R. Snow," 21.

46. Eliza R. Snow, *Poems: Religious, Historical, and Political* (1856), 148–49.

Chapter 5

1. Emmeline B. Wells, Clarissa S. Williams, and Julina L. Smith, "Resolutions of Relief Society," *Woman's Exponent*, Nov. 1913, 79.

2. 1 Corinthians 13:8; Moroni 7:46; see also General Board Minutes, 1842–2007, July 3, 1913, Church History Library.

3. Joseph Smith, in Relief Society Minute Book, Nauvoo, Illinois, June 9, 1842, Church History Library, 63.

4. Moroni 7:47.

5. Emmeline B. Wells, Clarissa S. Williams, and Julina L. Smith, "Epistle to the Relief Society Concerning These War Times," *Relief Society Magazine,* July 1917, 364.

6. See Moroni 7:46–47.

7. Joseph F. Smith, in Minutes of the General Board of Relief Society, Mar. 17, 1914, Church History Library, 54–55.

8. In "Notes from the Field," *Relief Society Magazine,* Sept. 1917, 512.

9. Emmeline B. Wells, "The Grain Question," Relief Society Bulletin, Sept. 1914, 1–2.

10. Amy Brown Lyman, "Social Service Work in the Relief Society, 1917–1928," typescript, Church History Library, 2.

11. Clarissa S. Williams, in "Relief Society Gives Hard Job to General Head," *Deseret News,* Sept. 23, 1925, section 2, page 1.

12. Gladys Robison Winter, in *The Life and Family of Louise Yates Robison,* comp. Gladys Robison Winter, Church History Library.

13. See Evelyn Hodges Lewis, interview by Loretta Hefner, Sept. 1979, transcript, Church History Library.

14. Louise Y. Robison, "Officers' Meeting," *Relief Society Magazine,* May 1935, 272.

15. Heber J. Grant, in Conference Report, Oct. 1936, 3.

16. Thomas S. Monson, "Guiding Principles of Personal and Family Welfare," *Ensign,* Sept. 1986, 5.

17. Harold B. Lee, "Place of the Relief Society in the Church Security Plan," *Relief Society Magazine,* Mar. 1937, 143; punctuation standardized.

18. Joseph L. Wirthlin, "Relief Society—An Aid to the Bishops," *Relief Society Magazine,* June 1941, 417.

19. "Memo of Suggestions," 1–6, Church Union Board Executive Committee Minutes, Church History Library.

20. Amy Brown Lyman, in Mayola R. Miltonberger, *Fifty Years of Relief Society Social Services* (1987), 2; capitalization standardized.

21. Boyd K. Packer, unpublished manuscript.

22. Maria Speidel, in "Notes from the Field," *Relief Society Magazine,* Feb. 1946, 123.

23. John Zippro, "Life Story of John Zippro," unpublished manuscript, quoted in Jill Mulvay Derr, Janath Russell Cannon, and Maureen Ursenbach Beecher, *Women of Covenant: The Story of Relief Society* (1992), 301–2.

24. Eva M. Gregerson, in "Notes from the Field," *Relief Society Magazine,* Feb. 1946, 118.

25. Hugh B. Brown, in "Notes from the Field," *Relief Society Magazine,* Oct. 1944, 591–92.

26. See Hedwig Biereichel, in Roger P. Minert, *In Harm's Way: East German Saints in World War II* (2009), 209.

27. See Jennifer A. Heckmann, in Nathan N. Waite, "Steadfast German Saints," *BYU Magazine,* Winter 2010, 57.

28. Amy Brown Lyman, *In Retrospect* (1945), 160–61.

29. Moroni 7:46–47.

Chapter 6

1. Eliza R. Snow, in Weber Stake Relief Society Minutes, Oct. 30, 1877, Church History Library, 27–28.

2. Belle S. Spafford, Marianne Sharp, and Gertrude Garff, "The New Year," *Relief Society Magazine,* Jan. 1947, 3.

3. Boyd K. Packer, in Conference Report, Apr. 1998, 94–95; or *Ensign,* May 1998, 72.

4. Boyd K. Packer, "The Circle of Sisters," *Ensign,* Nov. 1980, 109.

5. Henry B. Eyring, "The Enduring Legacy of Relief Society," *Ensign,* Nov. 2009, 124–25.

6. Boyd K. Packer, "The Circle of Sisters," 110.

7. Boyd K. Packer, in Conference Report, Apr. 1998, 97; or *Ensign,* May 1998, 74.

8. George Albert Smith, "Address to Members of Relief Society," *Relief Society Magazine,* Dec. 1945, 717.

9. See Belle S. Spafford, "A Relief Society Building to Be Erected," *Relief Society Magazine,* Dec. 1945, 751–53.

10. Belle S. Spafford, "Joy in Full Measure," *Relief Society Magazine,* Nov. 1948, 725.

11. David O. McKay, "Dedicatory Prayer of the Relief Society Building," *Relief Society Magazine,* Dec. 1956, 789.

12. Boyd K. Packer, in Conference Report, Oct. 1978, 10; or *Ensign*, Nov. 1978, 8–9.

13. Belle S. Spafford, interview by Jill Mulvay [Derr], Jan. 20, 1976, transcript, Church History Library, 127.

14. Belle S. Spafford, *A Woman's Reach* (1974), 98; paragraphing altered.

15. Silvia H. Allred, "Every Woman Needs Relief Society," *Ensign*, Nov. 2009, 115–16.

16. See Olga Kovářová Campora, "Fruits of Faithfulness: The Saints of Czechoslovakia," in *Women Steadfast in Christ* (1992), 141–46.

17. Spencer W. Kimball, "The Role of Righteous Women," *Ensign*, Nov. 1979, 103–4.

18. Elaine L. Jack, interview by Julie B. Beck, Feb. 10, 2009, transcript, Church History Library; punctuation standardized.

19. Elaine L. Jack, interview by Julie B. Beck, Feb. 10, 2009; capitalization and punctuation standardized.

20. Thomas S. Monson, "The Mighty Strength of Relief Society," *Ensign*, Nov. 1997, 95.

21. Julie B. Beck, "Fulfilling the Purpose of Relief Society," *Ensign*, Nov. 2008, 110.

22. Boyd K. Packer, "The Circle of Sisters," 109.

23. Boyd K. Packer, in Conference Report, Apr. 1998, 95; or *Ensign*, May 1998, 72.

24. Boyd K. Packer, "The Circle of Sisters," 110.

25. Thomas S. Monson, "Charity Never Faileth," *Ensign*, Nov. 2010, 124–25; see also Bible Dictionary, "Charity"; Moroni 7:46–47.

Chapter 7

1. Eliza R. Snow, "How Great the Wisdom and the Love," *Hymns*, no. 195.

2. See Luke 15:3–7.

3. See 3 Nephi 11:13–17; 17:5–25.

4. Julie B. Beck, "Relief Society: A Sacred Work," *Ensign*, Nov. 2009, 113.

5. Relief Society Minute Book, Nauvoo, Illinois, July 28, 1843, Church History Library, 101.

6. Joseph F. Smith, "Address of President Joseph F. Smith," *Woman's Exponent*, May 1903, 93; see also *Teachings of Presidents of the Church: Joseph F. Smith* (1998), 186–87.

7. Eliza R. Snow, in Relief Society Minutes, Sixth Ward, Salt Lake Stake, Aug. 16, 1868, Church History Library, 16; spelling and capitalization standardized.

8. Eliza R. Snow, in Mt. Pleasant North Ward Relief Society Minutes, Aug. 7, 1880, Church History Library, 56; capitalization standardized.

9. Sarah M. Kimball, in 15th Ward Relief Society Minutes, 1868–1873, Church History Library; punctuation standardized.

10. Jane Richards, in "R. S. Reports," *Woman's Exponent*, Sept. 1907, 24.

11. Minutes of General Board of Relief Society, Apr. 19, 1944, Church History Library, 39–40.

12. Belle S. Spafford, interview by Jill Mulvay [Derr], Dec. 1, 1975, transcript, Church History Library.

13. Belle S. Spafford, interview by Jill Mulvay [Derr], Dec. 8, 1975, transcript, Church History Library.

14. Henry B. Eyring, "The Enduring Legacy of Relief Society," *Ensign*, Nov. 2009, 123.

15. Julie B. Beck, "'Strengthen Thy Stakes': Strong and Immovable in Faith," in *Awake, Arise, and Come unto Christ: Talks from the 2008 BYU Women's Conference* (Deseret Book, 2009), 86–87; Portuguese translation revised.

16. Joseph Smith, in Relief Society Minute Book, Nauvoo, Illinois, Apr. 28, 1842, 38.

17. Spencer W. Kimball, "Small Acts of Service," *Ensign*, Dec. 1974, 5.

18. Thomas S. Monson, in Conference Report, Oct. 2009, 84; or *Ensign*, Nov. 2009, 86.

19. Dieter F. Uchtdorf, "Happiness, Your Heritage," *Ensign*, Nov. 2008, 120.

20. Spencer W. Kimball, "A Vision of Visiting Teaching," *Ensign*, June 1978, 24; see also Doctrine and Covenants 20:53–54.

21. Camilla Kimball, in Caroline Eyring Miner and Edward L. Kimball, *Camilla: A Biography of Camilla Eyring Kimball* (1980), 175.

22. Cathie Humphrey, in "Strong Hands and Loving Hearts," *Ensign*, Dec. 2004, 36–37.

23. Quoted by Mary Ellen Smoot, in interview by Julie B. Beck, May 20, 2009, transcript, Church History Library.

24. "Strong Hands and Loving Hearts," 39.

25. Spencer W. Kimball, "A Vision of Visiting Teaching," 24–25.

26. In Virginia U. Jensen, "Ripples," *Ensign*, Nov. 2000, 94.

27. Mary Ellen Smoot, in Conference Report, Oct. 1997, 13–14; or *Ensign*, Nov. 1997, 12.

28. Spencer W. Kimball, "A Vision of Visiting Teaching," 26.

29. Elaine Reiser Alder, "Visiting Teaching: The Multiplier Effect," *Ensign*, Mar. 1985, 19.

30. Elaine L. Jack, in Jaclyn W. Sorensen, "Visiting Teaching—Giving Selfless Service in a Loving

Sisterhood," *Church News,* Mar. 7, 1992, 5.

31. Vivien D. Olson, "The Visiting Teacher Who Made a Difference," *Church News,* May 15, 1982, 2.

32. Hope Kanell Vernon, "The Visiting Teacher Who Made a Difference," *Church News,* June 12, 1982, 2.

33. Barbara W. Winder, "Striving Together: A Conversation with the Relief Society General Presidency," *Ensign,* Mar. 1985, 12.

34. Robyn Romney Evans, "In the Vineyard," *Ensign,* Mar. 2004, 21–23.

35. Lorenzo Snow, in "Prest. Snow to Relief Societies," *Deseret Evening News,* July 9, 1901, 1; quoting James 1:27.

Chapter 8

1. Moses 1:39.

2. Dallin H. Oaks, in Conference Report, Apr. 1992, 51; or *Ensign,* May 1992, 36.

3. John A. Widtsoe, *Priesthood and Church Government* (1939), 83.

4. Elaine L. Jack, in Conference Report, Oct. 1996, 105; or *Ensign,* Nov. 1996, 76–77.

5. Sheri L. Dew, in Conference Report, Oct. 2001, 13; or *Ensign,* Nov. 2001, 13; quoting Doctrine and Covenants 109:22.

6. Elizabeth Ann Whitney, "A Leaf from an Autobiography," *Woman's Exponent,* Sept. 1, 1878, 51.

7. Elizabeth Ann Whitney, "A Leaf from an Autobiography," *Woman's Exponent,* Aug. 1, 1878, 33.

8. Joseph Smith, in Relief Society Minute Book, Nauvoo, Illinois, Apr. 28, 1842, Church History Library, 36.

9. Articles of Faith 1:7.

10. Amanda Barnes Smith, in Edward W. Tullidge, *The Women of Mormondom* (1877), 124, 128; see also *Our Heritage: A Brief History of The Church of Jesus Christ of Latter-day Saints* (1996), 47–48; the owner of the mill was a man named Jacob Hawn.

11. Elizabeth Ann Whitney, "A Leaf from an Autobiography," *Woman's Exponent,* Aug. 1, 1878, 33.

12. Joseph Smith, quoted by Mercy Fielding Thompson, in "Recollections of the Prophet Joseph Smith," *Juvenile Instructor,* July 1, 1892, 400.

13. Doctrine and Covenants 95:8.

14. Doctrine and Covenants 97:28.

15. Doctrine and Covenants 97:13–14.

16. Doctrine and Covenants 124:28, 40.

17. Elizabeth Ann Whitney, "A Leaf from an Autobiography," *Woman's Exponent,* Feb. 15, 1879, 191.

18. See Doctrine and Covenants 84:19–22.

19. Joseph Fielding Smith, "Relief Society—an Aid to the Priesthood," *Relief Society Magazine,* Jan. 1959, 5–6.

20. Russell M. Nelson, in Conference Report, Apr. 2006, 38; or *Ensign,* May 2006, 37.

21. Richard G. Scott, "The Doctrinal Foundation of the Auxiliaries," *Worldwide Leadership Training Meeting,* Jan. 10, 2004, 5.

22. Dallin H. Oaks, in Conference Report, Apr. 1992, 51; or *Ensign,* May 1992, 37; quoting 1 Corinthians 11:11.

23. Dallin H. Oaks, in Conference Report, Apr. 1992, 51; or *Ensign,* May 1992, 37; quoting Doctrine and Covenants 14:7.

24. See Doctrine and Covenants 68:25–28.

25. Bruce R. McConkie, in Conference Report, Sydney Australia Area Conference 1976, 34; quoting Moses 5:11.

26. "The Family: A Proclamation to the World," page 167 in this book.

27. Dallin H. Oaks, in Conference Report, Oct. 2005, 24, 26, 28; or *Ensign,* Nov. 2005, 24, 26–27.

28. Unpublished manuscript; author's name withheld.

29. Boyd K. Packer, in Conference Report, Apr. 1998, 95–96; or *Ensign,* May 1998, 72–73; quoting Doctrine and Covenants 107:5 and Joseph Smith, in Sarah M. Kimball, "Auto-biography," *Woman's Exponent,* Sept. 1, 1883, 51.

30. Doctrine and Covenants 38:27.

31. Joseph Smith, in Relief Society Minute Book, Nauvoo, Illinois, Mar. 30, 1842, 22.

32. Eliza R. Snow, in Relief Society Minutes, Eleventh Ward, Salt Lake Stake, Mar. 3, 1869, Church History Library.

33. Bathsheba W. Smith, "Official Announcement," *Woman's Exponent,* Jan. 1, 1902, 68.

34. Henry B. Eyring, "The Enduring Legacy of Relief Society," *Ensign,* Nov. 2009, 123.

35. Barbara W. Winder, interview by Susan W. Tanner, Jan. 3, 2011, transcript, Church History Library, 1.

36. Barbara W. Winder, interview by Susan W. Tanner, Jan. 3, 2011, 1.

37. Doctrine and Covenants 6:32.

38. Thomas S. Monson, in Conference Report, Oct. 1992, 68; or *Ensign,* Nov. 1992, 48–49.

39. Spencer W. Kimball, "Relief Society—Its Promises and Potential," *Ensign,* Mar. 1976, 4.

40. Joseph Fielding Smith, "Relief Society—an Aid to the Priesthood," 5.

41. Gordon B. Hinckley, in Conference Report, Oct. 1996, 90–91; or *Ensign*, Nov. 1996, 67–68.

Chapter 9

1. Gordon B. Hinckley, "Stand Strong against the Wiles of the World," *Ensign*, Nov. 1995, 100.

2. "The Family: A Proclamation to the World," pages 166–67 in this book.

3. Gordon B. Hinckley, quoted in "Inspirational Thoughts," *Ensign*, Aug. 1997, 5.

4. Barbara Thompson, "I Will Strengthen Thee; I Will Help Thee," *Ensign*, Nov. 2007, 117.

5. Bonnie D. Parkin, "Parents Have a Sacred Duty," *Ensign*, June 2006, 93.

6. Gordon B. Hinckley, "Stand Strong against the Wiles of the World," 101.

7. James E. Faust, "The Grand Key-Words for the Relief Society," *Ensign*, Nov. 1996, 94; capitalization standardized.

8. Gordon B. Hinckley, "Stand Strong against the Wiles of the World," 100.

9. "The Family: A Proclamation to the World," page 166 in this book.

10. Julie B. Beck, "Teaching the Doctrine of the Family," *Ensign*, Mar. 2011, 12.

11. See Doctrine and Covenants 138:38–39; Moses 5:10–12.

12. See Genesis 27–28; see also Julie B. Beck, "Teaching the Doctrine of the Family," 16.

13. See 1 Kings 17:8–24.

14. See Alma 56:47–48.

15. See Luke 2:40–52.

16. See Doctrine and Covenants 68:25–28; 93:36–48; 131:1–3.

17. Eliza R. Snow, "An Address," *Woman's Exponent*, Sept. 15, 1873, 63.

18. Zina D. H. Young, in "First General Conference of the Relief Society," *Woman's Exponent*, Apr. 15, 1889, 172.

19. Joseph F. Smith, in *Deseret Weekly*, Jan. 9, 1892, 71; see also *Teachings of Presidents of the Church: Joseph F. Smith* (1998), 31–32.

20. Zina D. H. Young, in "Relief Society Jubilee," *Woman's Exponent*, Apr. 1, 1892, 140.

21. Zina D. H. Young, in "First General Conference of the Relief Society," 172.

22. Joseph F. Smith, in Minutes of Relief Society General Board, Mar. 17, 1914, 50–51; as quoted in *Teachings of Presidents of the Church: Joseph F. Smith* (1998), 186.

23. Sheri L. Dew, "Are We Not All Mothers?" *Ensign*, Nov. 2001, 97.

24. Bonnie D. Parkin, "Parents Have a Sacred Duty," 97.

25. Barbara W. Winder, in "Enriching and Protecting the Home," *Ensign*, Mar. 1986, 20.

26. Belle S. Spafford, interview by Jill Mulvay [Derr], Mar. 8, 1976, transcript, Church History Library, 238.

27. M. Russell Ballard, in Conference Report, Apr. 2010, 17; or *Ensign*, May 2010, 18.

28. See Sheri L. Dew, "Are We Not All Mothers?" 96–98.

29. Julie B. Beck, in Conference Report, Oct. 2007, 81; or *Ensign*, Nov. 2007, 76–77.

30. Howard W. Hunter, "To the Women of the Church," *Ensign*, Nov. 1992, 96.

31. Message from the First Presidency, in Conference Report, Oct. 1942, 12; read by J. Reuben Clark Jr.

32. Message from the First Presidency, in Conference Report, Oct. 1942, 12–13; read by J. Reuben Clark Jr.

33. Barbara B. Smith, *A Fruitful Season* (1988), 55.

34. George W. Cornell, "Homemakers Get a Boost," *Fresno [California] Bee*, Apr. 5, 1978, C-5; quoted in Jill Mulvay Derr, Janath Russell Cannon, and Maureen Ursenbach Beecher, *Women of Covenant: The Story of Relief Society* (1992), 361.

35. See Susan W. Tanner, "Strengthening Future Mothers," *Ensign*, June 2005, 20.

36. David O. McKay quoting J. E. McCulloch, *Home: The Savior of Civilization* (1924), 42; in Conference Report, Apr. 1935, 116.

37. Harold B. Lee, "Be Loyal to the Royal within You," in *Speeches of the Year: BYU Devotional and Ten-Stake Fireside Addresses 1973* (1974), 91; see also *Teachings of Presidents of the Church: Harold B. Lee* (2000), 134.

38. Spencer W. Kimball, in Conference Report, Oct. 1980, 3–4; or *Ensign*, Nov. 1980, 4.

39. James E. Faust, in Conference Report, Apr. 2003, 70; or *Ensign*, May 2003, 68.

40. Gordon B. Hinckley, "Standing Strong and Immovable," *Worldwide Leadership Training Meeting*, Jan. 10, 2004, 20.

41. See Spencer W. Kimball, in Conference Report, Oct. 1971, 152–56; or *Ensign*, Dec. 1971, 36–39.

42. Gordon B. Hinckley, "Stand Strong against the Wiles of the World," 101.

43. Spencer W. Kimball, "Privileges and Responsibilities of Sisters," *Ensign,* Nov. 1978, 103.

44. Gordon B. Hinckley, "Stand Strong against the Wiles of the World," 101.

Chapter 10

1. Joseph Smith, in Relief Society Minute Book, Nauvoo, Illinois, Apr. 28, 1842, Church History Library, 38; spelling, punctuation, and capitalization standardized as needed in all excerpts from this minute book.

2. Mary Ellen Smoot, "Rejoice, Daughters of Zion," *Ensign,* Nov. 1999, 92–93.

3. M. Russell Ballard, "Women of Righteousness," *Ensign,* Apr. 2002, 69.

4. Joseph Smith, in Relief Society Minute Book, Nauvoo, Illinois, Apr. 28, 1842, 38.

5. Henry B. Eyring, "The Enduring Legacy of Relief Society," *Ensign,* Nov. 2009, 121.

6. See Athelia T. Woolley, with Athelia S. Tanner, "Our Five-Generation Love Affair with Relief Society," *Ensign,* June 1978, 37–39.

7. Henry B. Eyring, "The Enduring Legacy of Relief Society," 124–25.

8. Hebrews 12:1–2.

9. Doctrine and Covenants 138:39.

10. Eliza R. Snow, "Speech by E. R. Snow," *Woman's Exponent,* May 1, 1891, 167; capitalization standardized.

11. See Lynne Christy, "Now It's My Turn," *Ensign,* Mar. 1992, 25–27.

12. Joseph F. Smith, in Minutes of the General Board of Relief Society, Mar. 17, 1914, Church History Library, 54–55.

13. Esther 4:14.

14. Nehemiah 6:3.

15. 1 Nephi 14:14.

16. Emma Smith, in Relief Society Minute Book, Nauvoo, Illinois, Mar. 17, 1842, 12.

17. Doctrine and Covenants 25:1, 10, 13.

18. Joseph Smith, in Relief Society Minute Book, Nauvoo, Illinois, Apr. 28, 1842, 38–39.

List of Visuals

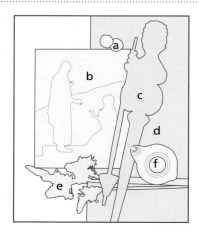
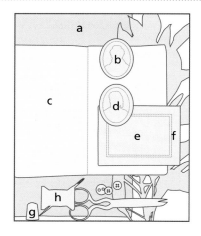

c. 1830s manuscript copy of the Book of Commandments and Revelations, which contained a record of revelations given through the Prophet Joseph Smith. Most of these revelations are now included in the Doctrine and Covenants.

d. Detail from *Emma Hale Smith,* by Lee Greene Richards. © 1941 IRI.

e. *Nauvoo, Illinois, 1859,* by John Schroder. © IRI.

f. Frame courtesy Church History Museum.

g. Buttons and thimble courtesy International Society Daughters of Utah Pioneers.

h. Pioneer needle, thread, and scissors courtesy Church History Museum.

Chapter 3

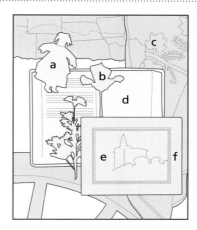

a. Pioneer doll courtesy International Society Daughters of Utah Pioneers.

b. Sego lily, an emblem of Relief Society. Early Utah settlers ate sego lily bulbs during a time of extreme hunger.

c. Pioneer quilt courtesy Church History Museum.

d. Icelandic hymnbook courtesy International Society Daughters of Utah Pioneers.

e. *Nauvoo Temple,* by Jon McNaughton. © Jon McNaughton.

f. Frame courtesy Church History Museum.

Page 35   *Wash Day on the Plains,* by Minerva K.
           Teichert. 1938. Courtesy Brigham Young
           University Museum of Art. All rights
           reserved. Do not copy.

Page 36   Detail from *Elizabeth H. Jackson: Pioneer
           Mother,* by Megan Rieker.

Page 37   Detail from *Pioneer Garden,* by VaLoy Eaton.
           © VaLoy Eaton. Courtesy Zions Bank. Do not
           copy.

Chapter 4

Page 4

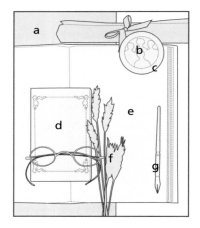

a. Shawl courtesy International Society
Daughters of Utah Pioneers.

b. Photograph of members of a graduating
class of the Relief Society Nursing School.
Courtesy International Society Daughters of
Utah Pioneers.

c. Frame courtesy International Society
Daughters of Utah Pioneers.

d. Facsimile reprint of 1852 German Book of
Mormon.

e. Relief Society Minute Book, Nauvoo,
Illinois, facsimile. Courtesy Church History
Museum. (See page 42.)

f. Wheat, an emblem of Relief Society.
(See pages 52–54.)

g. Fountain pen courtesy International
Society Daughters of Utah Pioneers.

Page 42   Detail from *Eliza R. Snow.* Courtesy Church
           History Museum.

Page 44   *Eliza Snow Instructs Relief Society Sisters,* by
           Michael T. Malm. © Michael T. Malm.

Page 46   Detail from *Prayer,* by Walter Rane. © Walter
           Rane.

Page 49   Detail from *Sabbath Study,* by Sheri Lynn
           Boyer Doty. © IRI. Courtesy Sheri Lynn
           Boyer Doty.

Page 50   *Spencer W. Kimball,* by Judith A. Mehr. © IRI.

           Brigham Young, by John Willard Clawson.

Page 56   Detail from *Zina Diantha Huntington Young.*
           Courtesy Church History Museum.

Page 59   Detail from *Rescue of the Lost Lamb,* by
           Minerva K. Teichert.

Chapter 5

Page 62

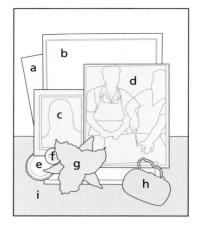

a. Note written on a postcard of the Beaver
West Ward Relief Society Hall, 1909.
Courtesy Church History Library.

b. Flyer created by the Relief Society general
board and delivered by visiting teachers,

asking for clothing donations for European Saints during World War II. Courtesy Church History Library.

c. *Christ's Image,* by Heinrich Hofmann. Courtesy C. Harrison Conroy Co., Inc.

d. Photograph courtesy Church History Library.

e. Relief Society seal used on a certificate of achievement issued by the Relief Society general board. Courtesy Church History Library.

f. Red Cross pin courtesy Church History Museum.

g. White trillium flower image copyright Gerald A. DeBoer, 2010. Used under license from Shutterstock.com.

h. Coin purse used by Harriet Barney Young. Courtesy International Society Daughters of Utah Pioneers.

i. Red paisley shawl courtesy Carma de Jong Anderson.

Chapter 6

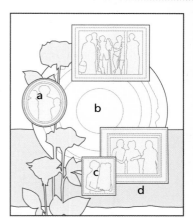

a. Photograph by Jeffrey D. Allred and Mike Terry. © *Deseret News.*

b. Needlepoint depicting the Relief Society seal.

c. Photograph of woman holding a Deseret Industries collection bag, 1940s. Courtesy Church History Library.

d. Pioneer lace courtesy Church History Museum. (See the statement by President Boyd K. Packer on page 99.)

Chapter 7

Page 104

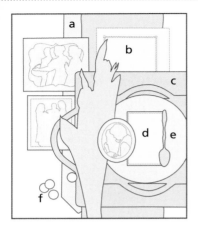

a. Friendship banner made by a group of women as a symbol of their friendship. Courtesy International Society Daughters of Utah Pioneers.

b. Visiting teaching record book courtesy Church History Museum.

c. Photograph of baskets © Joey Celis/Flickr/Getty Images.

d. Note card courtesy International Society Daughters of Utah Pioneers. It reads "The Lord Is on My Side."

e. Plate and spoon courtesy International Society Daughters of Utah Pioneers.

f. United States coins from the early 1900s, representing donations collected by visiting teachers. Courtesy Carma de Jong Anderson.

Page 105   Detail from *One by One,* by Walter Rane. Courtesy Church History Museum.

Page 107   *Pioneer Women,* by Julie Rogers. © Julie Rogers.

Page 114   Detail from *The Influence of Righteous Women,* by Julie Rogers. © 2009 Julie Rogers.

Page 116   Detail from *Visiting Teaching,* by Shannon Gygi Christensen. © 2006 Shannon Christensen.

Page 122   Painting by Keith Larson. © 1992 Keith Larson.

Page 123   Detail from *Lorenzo Snow,* by Lewis A. Ramsey. Courtesy Church History Museum.

Chapter 8

Page 126

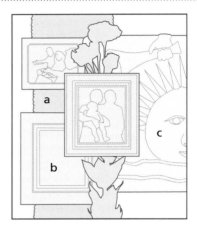

a. Sash made by Sarah Jane Casts Evans from silk she harvested from silkworms. Courtesy International Society Daughters of Utah Pioneers.

b. *Building the Kirtland Temple,* by Walter Rane, © IRI.

c. Sunstone used on the rebuilt Nauvoo Illinois Temple.

Page 130   Detail from *I'll Never Forsake,* by Julie Rogers. © Julie Rogers.

Page 133   Detail from *Joseph Fielding Smith,* by Shauna Cook Clinger. © 1983 IRI.

Page 135   *Adam and Eve Teaching Their Children,* by Del Parson. © 1978 IRI.

Page 136   Detail from *Barbara B. Smith,* by Cloy Kent. © IRI.

Page 140   Photograph of Barbara W. Winder © Busath Photography.

Chapter 9

Page 146

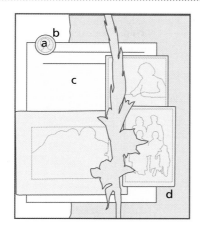

a. Portrait of Abbie H. Wells courtesy Church History Library.

b. Locket courtesy International Society Daughters of Utah Pioneers.

c. Samoan translation of "The Family: A Proclamation to the World."

d. Plaid blanket carded, spun, colored, and woven by Eliza R. Snow when she was a young woman. Courtesy International Society Daughters of Utah Pioneers.

Page 150 *Farewell, My Stripling Warrior,* by Del Parson. © Del Parson.

Page 151 *Rebekah at the Well,* by Michael Deas. © 1995 IRI.

Page 152 Photograph of Bonnie D. Parkin © Busath.com.

Page 158 Photograph of Julie B. Beck © Busath.com.

Chapter 10

Page 170

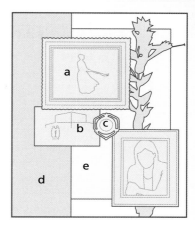

a. *Sunflowers and Buffalo Chips,* by Gary L. Kapp. Courtesy Church History Museum.

b. Photograph of women outside the Mesa Arizona Temple, 1920, by George Edward Anderson. Courtesy Church History Library.

c. Relief Society pin.

d. Pieced quilt designed by Cristina Franco, made for the Primary general presidency.

e. Page from Relief Society Minute Book, Nauvoo, Illinois, Mar. 17, 1842. Courtesy Church History Library. (See page 42.)

Page 173 *Turning Hearts to the Family,* by Anne Marie Oborn. © 1997 Anne Marie Oborn.

Page 175 Photograph © 2000 Steve Bunderson.

Page 179 Detail from *Queen Esther,* by Minerva K. Teichert. © William and Betty Stokes.

Important Events in the
History of Relief Society

Index

Church members, 128; on childless women finding ways to mother, 154

Disciples: among women in New Testament, xi, 3–6; among women today, xi, 7, 105, 180

Douglas, Ellen, gives and receives charity in times of need, 24–25

Dudley, Matilda, organizes women to care for needy American Indians, 36

E

Ensign magazine, 58

Esther, as an example of faith and courage, 180

Eve: and Adam, covenant relationship of, 135; and Adam, teaching their children together, 135, 150; and faithful daughters, worship God, 177

Eyring, Henry B.: on charity and the Atonement of Jesus Christ, 173–74; on respect between Relief Society sisters and priesthood holders, 140; on sharing charity, the heritage of Relief Society, 85–86, 173–74, 176; on the inspired pattern of visiting teaching, 110

F

Faith: and courage to meet challenges, 51; increasing, as a foundational principle in Relief Society, xi, xiii, 7, 17–18, 84, 155, 171; in Heavenly Father and Jesus Christ, xi, 3, 17–18, 29–32, 51, 70, 159, 173–74

Family: and the priesthood, 134–38; covenant relationship in, between husband and wife, 134–36; defending, 157–59; efforts of Joseph Smith and early Relief Society sisters to strengthen, 18–21; examples of righteousness in, 150,

162–65; proclamation to the world on, 166–67; providing temporal necessities for, 51; Relief Society teaching sisters' responsibilities in, 152–59; revelations on, 18–20; strengthening, as a foundational principle of Relief Society, xi, xiii, 7, 17, 18–21, 29, 41, 67–70, 75, 79, 84, 86–87, 96–97, 117–18, 134, 152–59, 171, 172; strengthening, as a fundamental purpose of the priesthood, 134, 152; strengthening, through temple ordinances, 20–21; teachings on, 149–51, 159–61; the foundation of a righteous life, 134, 149

Family, the: A Proclamation to the World: complete text of, 166–67; observations about, 147–49

Faust, James E.: on comfort for parents of wayward children, 160; on why the family proclamation was presented in general Relief Society meeting, 149

Fife, Veara, receives and gives service with her visiting teachers, 118

G

Gifts of the Spirit, women receiving, 130–31

God the Father. *See* Heavenly Father

Grant, Heber J.: and counselors, on motherhood as near to divinity, 157–58; and counselors, on principles of self-reliance, 71; on overcoming discouragement, 179; on the primary purpose of the welfare program, 72; reassures Louise Y. Robison after calling her to serve in a Relief Society general presidency, 71; supports the establishing of the Relief Society Social Service Department, 67

Gregersen, Eva M., on Danish Saints helping Norwegians during World War II, 77–78

H

Health care and medicine: sisters encouraged to learn, 54–55; training programs for nurses and nurses' aides, 68

Heavenly Father: eternal life with, 97; helps us accomplish great things, 179; knows His daughters, xii, 177; love of, 181; plan of, for our salvation and happiness, xii, 51, 143, 166, 171; praying to, 47, 55–56, 130–31; sealing ordinance binds families to, 134. *See also* Daughters of God; Faith

Helping those in need, as a foundational principle of Relief Society, xi, xiii, 7, 17, 21–25, 84, 155, 171. *See also* Charity; Visiting teaching

Hendricks, Drusilla Dorris, on sickness among Latter-day Saint pioneers, 32

Hinckley, Gordon B.: and counselors, on the home as the basis of a righteous life, 149; offers a blessing on women of the Church, 165; on doing the very best we can, 173; on service rendered, 113; on sisters' great capacity and essential place in Heavenly Father's plan, 142–43; on the need for the family proclamation, 148; on the strength of women working with priesthood brethren, 125; on women as guardians of the hearth, 148–49, 165; on women standing strong and immovable for righteousness, 160; reads the proclamation on the family in a general Relief Society meeting, 147–49

Holy Ghost: constant companionship of, 128; following the promptings of, in visiting teaching, 112–13, 114–16; gift of, 128; guidance and comfort from, 46; personal revelation through, 128

Home: as a center of strength, 155–57; examples of righteousness in, 162–65. *See also* Family

Homemaking: and nurturing, 157; art of, 156

Humphrey, Cathie, learns of her influence as a visiting teacher, 114

Hunter, Howard W.: on strengthening families, 157; on the divine birthright of daughters of God, 85

I

Indian student placement program, 75–76

Isaac and Rebekah, ensuring that covenants would not be lost, 150

J

Jack, Elaine L.: on blessings of the priesthood, 127–28; on promoting literacy, 96; on reaching out through visiting teaching, 119; on service rendered to celebrate the 150th anniversary of Relief Society, 95–96; on the sisterhood of Relief Society, 94

Jesus Christ: author and finisher of our faith, 177; following the example of, 105, 112; helping others feel the love of, 117; helping others follow, 95, 116–17; invites Martha and Mary to be His disciples, 3–4; mortal ministry of, 3–4; nurtured in childhood by Mary and Joseph, 150; Relief Society sisters' devotion to, 172; special love and concern of, for women, 3; teachings of, lead to happiness in family life, 147, 167; testimony of, guides our vision, 59. See also Atonement of Jesus Christ; Charity; Disciples; Faith

K

Kimball, Camilla, on her efforts as a visiting teacher, 113–14

Kimball, Presendia, on the lack of men to help Latter-day Saint pioneer companies, 31

Kimball, Sarah M.: and the beginnings of Relief Society, 11, 25; and the effort to store wheat, 53; on visiting teaching, 108

Kimball, Spencer W.: comparing visiting teaching with home teaching, 113; on cultivating Christlike attributes, 5; on glimpsing heaven in the lives of righteous Latter-day Saints, 162; on God meeting our needs through other people, 112; on growth of the Church because of the influence of sisters' example, 95; on Relief Society sisters studying the scriptures, 50; on resisting influences that weaken the family, 160; on the noble calling to be a righteous woman in the latter days, 145, 165; on the potential power of Relief Society, 142; on the powerful influence of righteous, articulate Relief Society sisters, 50–51, 95; on visiting teachers helping others follow the Savior, 116; on visiting teaching as a means to save souls, 117; on women who appreciate the past, xii

Kovářová, Olga, conversion and service of, 92–95

L

Lee, Harold B.: on becoming self-sustaining, 53; on temples as the only place on earth to receive the fulness of the blessings of the priesthood, 133; on the most important work being at home, 160; on unity among priesthood leaders and Relief Society leaders, 73

Liahona magazine, 58

Liljenquist, Emma Andersen, on learning about health care, 55–56

Lyman, Amy Brown: and changes in the original method of visiting teaching, 108–9; as director of the Relief Society Social Service Department, 67; emphasizes the need for mothers to be at home, 157; on experiences serving as a Relief Society leader, 79; on the greatness of Relief Society, 78; on the power of testimony, 79; on unity between Relief Society leaders and priesthood leaders, 75

Lyman, Elizabeth Partridge, on receiving and giving comfort at deaths of children, 32–33

M

Manifesto, 47–48

Martha and Mary, as disciples of Jesus Christ, xi, 3–4

Maternity hospital, 69

McConkie, Bruce R., on the covenant relationship between Eve and Adam, 135

McKay, David O.: gives dedicatory prayer for the Relief Society Building, 88; on no success compensating for failure at home, 160; on unity in the Church, 139

Medicine and health care, sisters encouraged to learn, 54–55

Monson, Thomas S.: on achieving the miraculous through faith, 91; on expressions of charity, 99–101; on objectives of the welfare program, 72–73; on serving as the Lord's hands on the earth, 103, 112; on the Relief Society's literacy efforts, 96; on women and men working together in response to Hurricane Andrew, 141–42

Mormon Battalion, 31

Mothering: a responsibility of all women, 156; childless women finding opportunities for, 154–55

Mothers, motherhood: defending, 157–59; influence on young warriors in the Book of Mormon, 150; part of women's eternal nature,

156; spiritual role of, 75; women encouraged to stay home, 75. *See also* Family

Motto of Relief Society: established, 63; followed by sisters in times of trial, 63–79. *See also* Charity

N

Nauvoo, exodus from, 29–30; Relief Society founded in, 12; service given in, 21–25; temple built in, 11

Nauvoo Temple: helping the builders of, 11; message written on the wall of, when Saints left Nauvoo, 30; thousands of Saints receive endowments and sealings in, 29

Nehemiah, as an example of faith and courage, 180–81

Nelson, Russell M., on families being sealed by priesthood power, 134

New Testament, women in, 3–6

Nurturing, and homemaking, 157

O

Oaks, Dallin H.: counsels with Barbara W. Winder on issues pertaining to women in the Church, 141; on his mother's leadership when his father died, 137; on the priesthood blessing women and men equally, 127; on the sacredness of marriage and family relationships, 134

Ordinances, blessings through, 15, 128–29. *See also* Covenants; Priesthood

P

Packer, Boyd K.: and wife, meet with circle of sisters in Czechoslovakia, 84–85, 98–99; on blessings that come to faithful Relief Society sisters, 99; on Indian student

placement program, 76; on sense of belonging to Relief Society, 138; on the influence of a ward or branch family, 87; on the protection of sisterhood in Relief Society, 81, 86; on women adopting virtues of Relief Society, 16

Parenting. *See* Family

Parkin, Bonnie D.: on developing charity at home, 152; on receiving strength at Relief Society meetings, 155–56; on the family proclamation, 148

Phebe, as a servant of the Church in New Testament times, 6

Pioneers: cleave to covenants upon leaving Nauvoo, 29–30; living conditions of, 30–35; service among, 32–37

Plural marriage: defended by early Latter-day Saint women, 46–49; United States government passes laws against, 46

Priesthood: blesses women and men equally, 127–28; blessings of, for faithful women, 15, 127–33; Relief Society organized under authority of, 12, 14–15, 99, 138; seals families eternally, 134; the foundation of a righteous life, 134

Priesthood quorums, compared with Relief Societies, 138, 152

Primary organization, 58

Privilege, living up to, 169, 171

Publications, 57–58

Public speaking, 49–51

R

Randall, Sally, finds comfort in baptism for the dead, 20–21

Rebekah and Isaac, ensuring that covenants would not be lost, 150

Reform. *See* Retrenchment

Relief Society: an essential part of the Restoration, 1, 7, 171; as a place of refuge and a place of influence, 81, 83, 84; beginnings of, 11, 171; compared with priesthood quorums, 138, 152; discontinued temporarily, 29; divine organization of, 7, 65–66, 171; doing something extraordinary, xi; early sisters' excitement to join, 15; exemplifying pure religion, 123; first meeting of, 12–14; healing mission of, 84; influence of, on sisters in wards and branches, 96–98; leaders in, serve under priesthood direction, 138; meetings of, teach charitable, practical, and family responsibilities, 155; organized under authority of and after the pattern of the priesthood, 12, 14–15, 99, 138; purposes of, xi, xiii, 7, 16–25, 84, 155, 171; reestablished, 41; teaching family responsibilities, 152

Relief Society Building, 88

Relief Society Magazine, 57–58

Retrenchment: definition of, 45; preached by Brigham Young and Eliza R. Snow, 45

Revelation, personal, individual sisters' ability to receive, 45–46, 158

Rich, Sarah, on Saints' blessings as they left Nauvoo, 30

Richards, Emily S., gains confidence as a public speaker, 49–50

Richards, Willard: attends the first Relief Society meeting, 12; present at the martyrdom of Joseph and Hyrum Smith, 29

Robison, Louise Y.: background of, 70–71; on appreciation for service provided by government, 72; on finding joy in serving God, 70; receives reassurance from Heber J. Grant after being called to serve in a Relief Society general presidency, 71

S

Sacred clothing, 134

Sandberg, Bobbie, received help from Relief Society president after an earthquake, 86–87

Scott, Richard G.: on home as the foundation of a righteous life, 134; on the priesthood supporting the family, 134

Scripture study, 50, 172

Sears, Athelia Call, passes the legacy of Relief Society to her family, 176

Self-reliance: developing, 51; cultivating, during the Great Depression, 70–72; examples of, among Relief Society sisters in the late 1800s, 51–58

Service. See Charity; Helping those in need; Visiting teaching

Sewing, 51–52

Silk, producing, 52

Sisterhood in Relief Society, 79, 83–101, 139, 155, 172

Sisters, single: are blessed as they keep their covenants, 136–38; preside in their homes, 137–38

Smith, Amanda Barnes, receives the gift of prophecy to care for her son, 130–31

Smith, Barbara B.: on defending the family and motherhood, 158–59; on Relief Society sisters following priesthood counsel and receiving inspiration, 136

Smith, Bathsheba W.: establishes mother education lessons, 153; on gaining a testimony of the restored gospel, 34; on trials and blessings of early Latter-day Saint pioneers, 33–34; on unity between women and men in the Church, 140

Smith, Emma: an example of charitable service, 24; chosen as first Relief Society president, 12–13; on her desire to be guided by revelation, 12; on mothers teaching their daughters, 19; on Relief Society doing something extraordinary, xi, 14; revelation for, 13–14

Smith, George Albert: counsels Belle S. Spafford to make her influence felt, 88–91; on happiness through service, 77; on Joseph Smith turning the key for the emancipation of womankind, 87

Smith, Hyrum, martyrdom of, 29

Smith, Joseph: encourages the Saints to help build the Nauvoo Temple, 11; instructions of, inspire early pioneer women, 34; instructs sisters on the purposes of Relief Society, 16–25; leads efforts to build the Kirtland Temple, 21; martyrdom of, 29; on angels associating with Relief Society sisters, 181; on blessings of the temple, 131–32; on duties of the Relief Society presidency, 13; on helping those in need, 22–23, 119; on organizing the Relief Society, 9, 12–15; on Relief Society as a restoration of an ancient pattern, 1, 7; on Relief Society as a select society, 15; on Relief Society as something better, 12; on Relief Society sisters' ability to act according to their sympathies, 16, 41, 112, 173; on Relief Society sisters living up to their privilege, 169, 171; on Relief Society sisters relieving the poor and saving souls, 17, 24, 63, 83; on searching the scriptures, 47; on the power of kindness, 23; on the revelation in D&C 25, 14; on unity in the Church, 139; on women being first and foremost in good works, 21–22; on women having feelings of charity, 172; on women receiving gifts of the Spirit, 130; priesthood restored through, 127; revelations to, on family responsibilities, 18–20

Smith, Joseph F.: on Relief Society leading the world in praiseworthy things, 65–66, 179–80; on Relief Society teaching family responsibilities, 153–54; on seeing Relief Society sisters serving a family in need, 106–7; on the divine nature of Relief Society, 7, 65–66; on the example of his mother, 151–52; on the protecting influence of his mother, 155

Smith, Joseph Fielding: on Relief Society being established by revelation, 13; on Relief Society helping faithful members gain eternal life, 97; on the relationship between the Relief Society and priesthood quorums, 142; on women receiving temple blessings, 133

Smith, Lucy Mack, on sisterhood in Relief Society, 25

Smith, Lucy Meserve: on providing service for early Saints arriving in the Salt Lake Valley, 36–37; on willingness to continue serving others, 37

Smith, Mary Fielding, example as a mother, 151–52

Smoot, Mary Ellen: and counselors, on what it means to be a daughter of God, 172; on Relief Society sisters helping others feel the Savior's love, 117; on the need for faithful visiting teachers, 118

Snow, Eliza R.: called as first Relief Society secretary, 16; called as second Relief Society general president, 44; called to help bishops establish Relief Societies in their wards, 42; called to instruct the sisters, 44; keeps minutes of early Relief Society meetings, 16–17; on following the example of Jesus Christ, 105; on heavenly record of service rendered, 83; on home as first priority, 151; on personal revelation, 45, 46; on Relief Society sisters expressing their thoughts, 49; on retrenchment, 45; on serving without need for public recognition, 42, 177; on sisters establishing fashions in clothing, 51–52; on sisters gaining an education in medicine, 54, 55;